Contemporary Issues in Ethics and Information Technology

Robert A. Schultz
Woodbury University, USA

D1529204

IRM Press
Publisher of innovative scholarly and professional
information technology titles in the cyberage
Hershey • London • Melbourne • Singapore

Acquisitions Editor:	Michelle Potter
Development Editor:	Kristin Roth
Senior Managing Editor:	Amanda Appicello
Managing Editor:	Jennifer Neidig
Copy Editor:	Jane Conley
Typesetter:	Diane Huskinson
Cover Design:	Lisa Tosheff
Printed at:	Yurchak Printing Inc.

Published in the United States of America by
      IRM Press (an imprint of Idea Group Inc.)
      701 E. Chocolate Avenue, Suite 200
      Hershey PA 17033-1240
      Tel: 717-533-8845
      Fax: 717-533-8661
      E-mail: cust@idea-group.com
      Web site: http://www.irm-press.com

and in the United Kingdom by
      IRM Press (an imprint of Idea Group Inc.)
      3 Henrietta Street
      Covent Garden
      London WC2E 8LU
      Tel: 44 20 7240 0856
      Fax: 44 20 7379 0609
      Web site: http://www.eurospanonline.com

Library of Congress Cataloging-in-Publication Data

Schultz, Robert A., 1942-
  Contemporary issues in ethics and information technology / Robert A. Schultz.
     p. cm.
  Summary: "This book uses general ethical principles as a basis for solutions to solving ethical problems in information technology use within organizations"--Provided by publisher.
  Includes bibliographical references and index.
  ISBN 1-59140-779-6 (hardcover) -- ISBN 1-59140-780-X (softcover) -- ISBN 1-59140-781-8 (ebook)
  1. Ethics. 2. Information technology. 3. Technology--Moral and ethical aspects. I. Title.
  BJ995.S38 2006
  174'.9004--dc22
                        2005020635

British Cataloguing in Publication Data
A Cataloguing in Publication record for this book is available from the British Library.

All work contributed to this book is new, previously-unpublished material. The views expressed in this book are those of the authors, but not necessarily of the publisher.

Contemporary Issues in Ethics and Information Technology

Table of Contents

Section II: Ethics and IT Professionals

Section III: Ethics and IT Users

Section IV. Ultimate Questions

Foreword

Being trained in history and philosophy and only involved with information technology as a "power user," I was feeling both honored and ill-prepared to undertake the task of writing this foreword. I have worked on the edges of information technology as a user of databases and a writer of Web pages for the courses I teach, but I am by no means an information technology professional. I have a bit more experience with the study of ethics, especially social ethics, but I am not by profession an ethicist. Upon further reflection, however, I believe that my position halfway between the two fields that inform this work, as a student of ethical theories and a creator of simple information technology, gives me a unique perspective on Dr. Schultz's work here. I have written a bit on the ethical and political impact of information technology as it relates to distance education and course structure. I have also been a colleague of Dr. Schultz' for almost 12 years and have discussed many of the issues here with him before. All of this gives me a good position from which to begin, for the ethical implications of information technology are issues about which all of us ought to be concerned.

Specifically, what I have found missing in my experience is a work that guides users, writers, managers, and developers through the maze of value questions that envelop work with and within information technology. In my own work writing Web pages for my university courses, I have had to determine the answer to such questions myself (or turn to Dr. Schultz for advice and debate). For example, how do I predetermine access? Should my pages be password protected or openly available? Should I learn Flash and Java in order to expand the possibilities (and bandwidth requirements) of the information I'm displaying, or should I make it as simple and as transparent as possible so even users of older technology and dial-up can easily access what I've created? Mundane questions for some, but they are important in my line of work for reaching students and a broader international audience.

Or I have asked myself, how should the information in these Web pages be presented? Should I use lists, trees, tables, multiple linked pages, and so forth? What are the educational implications of organizing data in certain patterns? Should the presentation be understandable only to initiates or should it be easily understandable even if you're not enrolled in the course? I have made my own decisions on these matters (open availability, low-bandwidth require-ments, simplified organization, ease of understandability), but I have made them after several attempts at other solutions, other combinations, and expe-rience with failure.

In the end, these are questions about the values of information technology, about the costs and benefits of the work and the world that information tech-nology creates. These are not technological questions, but ethical questions about how human beings treat each other within an environment mediated by information technology. To that end, Dr. Schultz has written a marvelous and informative work that combines reflections on the nature of Informational Tech-nology with its ethical implications.

He has made two significant contributions to the field herein. The first involves moving the problems of ethics and information technology beyond the usual nexus of provider-client relationships, contract obligations, and copyright in-fringement. By looking at the way information is organized, distributed, or-dered, and dispersed, Schultz has raised questions about the ethical effects of information technology on individuals and on society as a whole. By placing such questions within the framework of a quest for justice and equity, he holds up the work of information technology professionals to a higher calling than technocratic efficiency. Furthermore, he has placed all these questions in a context informed by philosophical and ethical reflections on technology itself, as well as information technology.

Such questions have usually been the province of cultural theorists, philoso-phers, or science fiction writers, and have generally been cautionary at best and dystopian at worst. Dr. Schultz, to the contrary, appreciates the liberating and developmental possibilities within information technology, while also high-lighting how such technologies can be used in limiting and regressive fashions. These insights have been developed through the second major contribution this book makes.

Dr. Schultz brings together two highly influential theorists of the 20th Century: the American John Rawls (who wrote, among other things, on justice) and the German Martin Heidegger (who wrote, among other things, on technology). In the first place, bridging the worlds of analytic (Anglo-American, logical, scientific) and continental (European, humanistic, phenomenological) philosophy is a daunting task only rarely completed successfully. In the second place, Rawls' theories of justice, of evaluating the requirements for making just decisions with minimal assumptions, seem worlds away from Heidegger's concern with our loss of meaning and the abstracted, dehumanized world created by technological development. Yet Dr. Schultz bridges these gaps, using each thinker's work to fill the lacunae in their own. It is remarkable work of intellectual synthesis and practical application.

Whatever your background or reason for opening this book—an information technology manager looking for solutions to certain dilemmas, a student in an information technology course exploring the limits of the field, or a theorist interested in the ethical implications of information technology—you will be challenged and provoked by the arguments in here. You will find many to disagree with (I found a few), but you will also find many more to agree with, and a few about which you had not even thought. It certainly helped me think through some of the problems I encounter in my everyday role as user and part-time writer, and I believe it will help you do so as well, wherever you come from in approaching this book. Be prepared for a stimulating, thought-provoking, and challenging journey. At the end, you will be glad you took the trip.

Douglas J. Cremer, PhD
Professor of History and Interdisciplinary Studies
Woodbury University, Burbank, CA

Preface

Information technology (IT) has caused and will continue to cause enormous changes in the ways we do things. Very often, the introduction of new technologies results in dramatic alterations in old ways of relating to each other. Examples range all the way from entirely new ways of meeting romantic partners to making travel arrangements; from new ways of connecting with suppliers to entirely new kinds of businesses. It is, therefore, only to be expected that IT produces new challenges and issues for us to deal with ethically. Issues about privacy, security, piracy, and ownership take on new aspects when applied to new IT applications. So far, in discussions of ethical issues of IT, these types of issues have been the most discussed. Yet other important issues that raise difficult ethical problems also need to be addressed, for example, the outsourcing of high-level jobs and the value of information technology itself.

I will be using a framework for ethical problems influenced very much by the late philosopher John Rawls. Rawls is regarded by many political theorists as the greatest social and political philosopher of the 20th century. His importance was perhaps signaled by the fact that his obituary appeared in the News and Review section of the *New York Times* rather than in the regular obituary section. He was my PhD thesis adviser at Harvard, so I had the chance to gain familiarity with his work. This book does not contain a full and accurate account of his work. Its intended audience is IT professionals and IT users who have ethical concerns. A full and accurate account of Rawls' work would take us into the convolutions of professional philosophy, which I intend to avoid.[1] This is very much a book of *applied* ethics, but I have tried my best to be faithful to the spirit of the ideals of Rawls' work.[2]

The basic idea is that ethical problems arise because there are conflicts between different interests. IT examples include: music downloaders vs. music rights owners; corporate managers or stockholders vs. outsourced professionals; spammers vs. e-mail users. These problems cannot be resolved on the level of individual interests alone. Higher level principles need to be applied. Very often, these higher level considerations are embodied in laws, but laws themselves need to be ethical—we need to know that laws themselves are just. Rawls' main contribution to ethics was a theory of justice based on the idea that justice means fairness to all concerned, plus a method for determining when this is so[3] (Rawls, 1999). As I worked on the various issues discussed in the book, I experienced once again the power of these ideas of Rawls. They are direct descendants of the founding ideas of the United States, so it is perhaps no wonder that they are so attractive.

In Section I, Ethics and IT—The Background, ethics is applied to information technology. Chapter I, Ethical Issues in Information Technology, considers three questions:

- What makes an issue an ethical issue?
- What features of information technology create new ethical issues?
- Who is to say what is right and wrong?

My answer to the question, "Who is to say what is right and wrong?" is the person with the most overall view using the highest level principles.

Chapter II, A Background in Ethical Theory, introduces the underlying ethical principles used in the rest of the book. The basis for deciding on ethical principles is the principle of higher level principles; it is rational to follow a higher level principle to resolve conflicts between lower level principles.

I present some classical theories of right action and a classical theory of value. Then I discuss how higher level ethical principles for institutions arise and outline the social contract theory of justice developed by John Rawls. The basic idea of a social contract is that a justly ordered society is one to which individuals can freely decide to obligate themselves. Rawls believes two principles of justice would be chosen to regulate institutions: Greatest Equal Liberty—all members of society have the greatest equal liberty possible, including fair equality of opportunity; and the Difference Principle—economic inequalities in society are justified by their making the least advantaged better off than if there were no inequality. Finally, Rawls' extension of his social contract theory to a transnational context is explained.

In Chapter III, The Context of IT Ethical Issues, ethical issues within organizations are seen to arise from three points of view: IT professionals, IT users, and general managers. I also discuss *partial compliance,* how to deal with cases where ethical principles are not being fully observed. How to deal with such cases turns out to be important in many of the following chapters.

In Section II, Ethics and IT Professionals, some IT ethical issues within organizations are considered from the point of view of the IT professional. Discussion in Chapter IV is based on traditional theories of right. Chapters V, VI, and VII rely on John Rawls' theory of justice.

In Chapter IV, Professional Duties, I begin by considering the nature of the IT profession and the special ethical duties of the IT professional. My position is that IT has developed a distinctive and robust set of professional ethical standards even without the benefit of formal credentialing and accreditation.

Since ethical behavior for the IT professional is also impacted by the ethics of people and institutions in his or her environment, the rest of the chapters in this part consider the justice of institutions impacting the IT professional. The theory of justice used is the social contract theory developed by John Rawls.

Economic justice is the major focus in Chapters V, Justice in a Market Economy, and Chapter VI, Trust Issues in a Market Economy. These chapters examine the ethical constraints necessary for justice in an efficient market economy. The basis for the discussion is Rawls' second principle of justice, the Difference Principle, which requires social institutions to be arranged to make the worst off in society as well off as possible. Topics discussed include monopoly, the "digital divide," trust in supply chain management and outsourcing, and dealing with unethical organizational behavior.

Chapter VII, Offshoring as an Ethical Issue, examines the justice of the practice of moving skilled IT jobs to lower wage countries. Rawls' extension of his principles of justice to transnational contexts, which he calls "the law of peoples," is the basis for my analysis. One major concern is that the safeguards of justice present internally in national economies are not automatically duplicated in transnational contexts.

In Section III, Ethics for IT Users, we turn to issues relating to the individual user of IT These issues include several much-discussed ethical issues such as privacy, security, copyright, and piracy. Some other less usual problems involving the individual are also discussed. These are issues that take on a different cast in an online environment, such as taxing Internet sales equitably and eliminating paper from transactions.

I include these issues here to give some idea of what a Rawlsian treatment of them would look like. I have not been able to include consideration of the very extensive discussions of these issues. Some of the ethical principles involved in this part are not discussed by Rawls, but I believe they are natural extensions of his principles. Of special ethical significance is a very strong individual right to privacy, formulated and discussed in Chapter VIII. The discussion of copyright in Chapter IX also turned out to be the most appropriate place to consider the ethical status of corporations, an issue Rawls does not directly consider.

The range of issues in Chapter X each require different treatment because of their special features. Sales tax is traditionally collected at the location of the infrastructure supporting the business, but there doesn't seem to be any way to apply this to Web-based transactions. Paperless transactions raise the issue of justice for those without access to computers. Spam raises free-speech issues. Finally, although the Internet seems to raise no new ethical issues concerning dating and sex, the difficulty in censoring the Internet does underline its contribution to realizing the first principle of justice—that of Greatest Equal Freedom, especially with respect to freedom of speech.

Section IV, Ultimate Questions, begins in Chapter XI with issues of how to value IT itself. These issues are considered from various points of view: I begin with the point of view of organizations and the economy and then consider the ultimate value of technology and IT from the point of view of the human species, the environment, and *being* itself.

The discussion of IT value from organizational and socioeconomic points of view builds from a discussion of the "productivity paradox" of the early 1990s. Because of the uncertainties involved in assessments of global socioeconomic value, this type of value assessment may not be useful to managers in organizations. Managers are, after all, concerned with whether they can realize value from particular projects. I discuss ways of realizing value in particular projects and barriers to realizing this value.

Chapters XII and XIII consider "ultimate" ethical questions of the value of technology from the point of view of humanity, the ecosystem, and *being* itself. Chapter XII first discusses the value of modern technology per se, and then Chapter XIII discusses to what extent conclusions about modern technology apply to information technology.

My analysis of modern technology is based on Heidegger's view of modern technology as an independent force in human existence, with its own point of view and its own ends, chiefly to build a new and incompatible order for the purpose of extracting and storing energy for later uses. The ends of technology are expressed in an ethical principle I call the Technology Principle. Two other ethical principles, the Species Survival Principle and the Ecosystem Principle, emerge from a discussion from the points of view of the species and the environment. I argue that these principles have priority over the Technology Principle. To establish this priority, ultimately one must take the point of view of *being* itself.

In the final chapter, I consider whether IT possesses the characteristics of modern technology. I conclude that the answer is quite different for IT hardware and IT applications. IT hardware is a part of modern technology, but IT applications are not. IT as application is not trying to replace the world, but rather to produce a useful simulation of the world, being in this respect like art. At the end, I discuss the ethical implications of these views for managers, the species, the ecosystem, and *being* itself.

Ethics can have two possible emphases: on *judgments* or on *agents.* A judgment emphasis in ethics results in judgments of the behavior or character of others. An agent emphasis in ethics provides guidance for an individual trying to decide what to do. This book has an agent emphasis. My aim is to have produced a book useful for dealing with practical ethical problems of IT— problems faced by professionals and users. But, in any case, ethical solutions must be based on higher level principles, because, in the end, this is the only way we can deal ethically and consistently with the rapidly changing environment presented to us by IT.

References

Rawls, J. (1999). *A theory of justice* (rev.ed.). Cambridge, MA: Harvard University Press.

Rogers, B. (2002). John Rawls. *The Guardian*, November 27.

Spinello, R., & Tavani, H. (2004). *Readings in cyberethics.* Sudbury, MA: Jones and Bartlett.

Endnotes

1   It seems to me that if Rawls' theory can't be understood without the substantial added complexity of professional philosophy, then it is probably not workable as a practical basis for ethics—or for society.

2   For a recent collection of professional philosophical work on ethics and IT, see Spinello and Tavani (2004).

3   Rogers (2002) is an obituary with an excellent summary of Rawls' work.

Acknowledgments

I would like to thank Woodbury University for providing sabbatical time for writing this book. I would especially like to thank my colleague Douglas Cremer for his insightful comments that I believe resulted in great improvement to many chapters. Eric Eldred deserves thanks for his helpful comments on Chapter IX. Endoh Toake and Yasushi Zenno initially supplied me with the central idea of the book. I would also like to thank my editors and reviewers at Idea Group Inc. for their helpful comments.

For their encouragement, I would like to thank David Rosen and my other colleagues at Woodbury University, my daughters Katie and Rebecca, and my ex-cousin-in-law Andrew Ross. Finally, thanks to my friend Steve Moore for his unwavering support.

Section I

Ethics and IT—
The Background

Chapter I

Ethical Issues in Information Technology

Most discussions of ethics and information technology focus on issues of professional ethics and issues of privacy and security.[1] Certainly these are important issues, But so are issues such as the offshoring of Information Technology (IT) jobs or the value of IT as a whole. But are they ethical issues, business issues, or economic issues?

What is Ethics?

Our first question is, therefore: *What makes an issue an ethical issue?* "Ethics" is currently a general term for concerns about what people should do. The term "ethics" comes from the Greek word *ethike* that means "character," and indeed the ancient Greeks conceived issues about what people should do in terms of impact upon character (Aristotle, 350 BCE). We still think this way when our concern is good reputation. Much professional ethics for IT consultants, for example, revolves around preserving and developing a good reputation for being the sort of person who will regularly do good work, make sure a project is done well, and the like. One's reputation is for being the kind of person who will consistently behave well, but good character is by no means our only concern with regard to what people should do. Bad actions and bad performance can be more important than any amount of good reputation if they are bad enough. People sometime surprise us when they act "out of character." On the other hand, it is our belief in enduring character that allows people to "coast on their (good) reputations." And IT firms affirm their belief in the enduring character of technical expertise when they hire previously convicted hackers like Kevin Mitnick.

Nowadays, "ethics" seems to be an inclusive term for concerns also referred to by "morality," "value," and "justice." Besides character and action, ethics in this inclusive sense is also concerned with the value or goodness of things and situations and with the justness of institutions (both formal and informal). In this book, the term "ethics" will be used in this inclusive sense.

To understand what is at stake here, let us now take a preliminary look at two issues concerning IT that may not seem to be ethical issues: the offshoring of IT jobs and the value of IT as a whole. It is important not to think of what is at stake here as purely a terminological issue—we call it ethics and you call it economics. The real question is: Why is it important that we treat an issue as an ethical issue? The basic idea is that ethical problems arise because they involve conflicts between different interests that cannot be resolved on the level of interests alone. Higher level principles need to be applied.

Consider the offshoring of IT jobs. There are at least three sets of conflicting interests: the corporations who save large amounts of money on labor costs; the offshore workers who receive better salaries in their home economies; and the United States workers who lose their jobs. Each of these parties has important considerations involving their own interests: the corporation for maximizing profits and shareholder return, the offshore workers for improving their income, and the U.S. workers for keeping their jobs. There are additional self-interested considerations for the corporation: Some jobs simply do not outsource well, even if the technical abilities of the workers in the two countries are the same (Ante, 2004). But even when all self-interested considerations are taken into account, there remains an ethical issue, an issue of justice. Defenders of offshoring maintain that free trade of jobs will make everyone better off in the long run.[2] This claim goes beyond considerations of self-interest and it may be true or false. There will be an extended discussion of this issue later in Chapter VII, Offshoring as an Ethical Issue, but for now it is enough to point out that jobs occur within a social and economic context, and it is within that context that economic inequalities are ethically justified. So why is offshoring of employment any more justified than offshoring of tax liabilities? It is clear in both cases that corporations benefit from the social and economic institutions that allow them to function in their home country. It might be expected that they make corresponding contributions to their home country even when they could do better otherwise.[3]

As I said, this issue is complex, and sorting out the relevant considerations will occupy a full chapter. Right now, it is important to see that this issue has a significant ethical component that needs to be addressed, and not because of terminology, but because there are conflicting interests involved that need to be addressed by higher level principles. On an institutional level, many such principles are laws, but the ethical component of such discussion is implied in the famous statement, "There ought to be a law." The ethical question behind this statement is "Ought there to be a law?" And even if there is a law, the ethical question is "Is it a just law?" And behind this question is a major theoretical question, "What is justice?"

In the late 20th Century, the philosopher John Rawls developed a theory of justice based on the idea that justice means fairness to all concerned, plus a method for determining when this is so (Rawls, 1999). The method is based on the idea that fair principles are principles that all members of society would acknowledge as binding to settle problems of conflicting interests. (Of course, this means that people have to leave aside their own particular interests in deciding which principles to acknowledge.) More detailed discussion appears in the next chapter, A Background in Ethical Theory, and in the several other chapters that apply Rawls' theory.[4] But for right now, we can see that justice is possible only between members of the same community, because within that community, they can see that the sacrifices of some contribute to everyone's well-being, even those who sacrifice. Perhaps a simple example would be paying for software licenses as opposed to copying software without paying license fees. Although this principle is accepted in Western countries, there continues to be widespread violation of this principle in Asian countries. At one time, China was notorious as a source for cheap copies of very expensive software. In these circumstances, we cannot appeal to the shared benefits and burdens of a common social contract that does not now exist. And until it exists, there is very little hope of addressing these violations as unjust or unethical and appealing to shared interests.[5]

So what is the significant difference between, on the one hand, corporations moving headquarters to low-tax countries and, on the other hand, taking an IT function across to China to have it performed for a fraction of the cost by a member of Chinese society working under Chinese social conditions, rules, and expectations? To say that somehow all will be better off someday in the offshoring case seems no more plausible than saying that corporations moving their headquarters offshore to low-tax countries will somehow make everyone better off someday. Or to say that underdeveloped countries not collecting license fees will somehow make everyone better off someday. There is no question that some corporations are better off right now. But claims that more than their own corporate interests are served are far from obviously true and need the fuller examination we will give them later. This is the ethical content of the issue of offshoring of IT jobs.

The Value of IT

The second sample issue, the value of IT as a whole, may seem to be an economic rather than an ethical issue, but again, we need to look beyond mere terminology. Value depends on interests from a point of view. A valuable object is typically one that performs its function well. For example, good antivirus software must prevent and destroy viruses; a good keyboard cleaner must clean keyboards well, and so on.[6] Very often, we simply assume that the point of view from which value is to be evaluated is our own or that of our group. Most disagreements about value are in fact disagreements about the appropriate point of view to use for evaluation. However, within a point of view, there is nothing especially subjective about value. Whether something is valuable from a point of view is a matter of fact.

Now what makes the question of the value of IT as a whole an ethical question is the difficulty in determining the appropriate point of view (with its interests) from which to determine value. Clearly it needs to be a general point of view, but how general and whose? Computer users? Organizational users? Societies? Humanity as a whole? The question transcends clearly definable sets of interests and, thus, becomes for us an ethical question. At very least, we need to look at it from the point of view of societies using IT. From this point of view, we need to consider whether the background social institutions are just. In a totalitarian regime, the use of IT to oppress its citizens would be valuable to the totalitarian regime, but not to the victims of oppression.

IT and New Ethical Issues

So the range of ethical issues important for IT is perhaps broader than one might have thought. But are the issues really any different from other ethical issues? Does IT itself produce circumstances that don't fit into preexisting ethical categories? Our second question is: *What features of Information Technology create new ethical issues?*

Right now, the definition of "information technology" may seem obvious. But the term is actually fairly new and dates from about 1990—just about the same time that networked computers and the Internet came into widespread usage. Here is a definition from whatis.com (www.whatis.techtarget.com):

IT (Information Technology) is all forms of technology used to create, store, exchange, and use information in its various forms (business data, voice conversations, still images, motion pictures, multimedia presentations, and other forms, including those not yet conceived).

The last few words of this definition indicate why we cannot expect a definitive answer to this question. There will be new uses of information technology and its successors that will allow new actions, new responses, new institutions, and new relations to each other. We already know that the ability to process and store information in radically new ways can result in such changes. But some of the most striking uses of information technology have not arrived in a predictable way in the past, nor should we expect them to arrive predictably in the future.

What we can expect is that new uses will be built on four basic features of information technology:

- *Speed* of information processing;
- Unlimited size of information *storage* capacity;
- *Availability* of information at any location (connectivity); and
- Easy *reproduction* of digital information.

These features combine in many different ways to produce the various applications of IT that give rise both to new benefits and to new ethical problems. Speed by itself enables simulations of complex phenomena such as weather and chemical reactions. Speed also enables the ability to copy detailed documents and pictures quickly and accurately. Storage plus speed (of retrieval) enables the contents of huge libraries to be compressed to a few disks. The storage feature of IT involves both a great amount of information and a decreasingly small space in which to store the information. Storage helps with the availability of information at any location, but the major factor is universal connectivity through the Internet and the World Wide Web. Essentially anyone with an Internet connection can, in principle, access information on any other connected computer in the world. Easy reproduction allows new (and sometimes unwelcome) ways of sharing material previously much harder to disseminate, such as digitized music and movies.

But just as new and unpredictable uses of information technology arise with some regularity, so do new and unpredictable ethical problems. Information Technology is embedded in a human world of actions, relations, and institutions, and it is to be expected that its interaction with that world would not yield predictable ethical problems—or predictable solutions either.

The phenomenon of Napster provides striking confirmation of this observation. The brilliant and revolutionary idea of distributed storage on millions of machines with no centralized profit-taking was defeated by centralized profit-takers. This result was not predictable. The record (and movie) companies might have ended up taking the same line as they had with cassette audio tapes and VCRs. After an initial attempt to block any copying, they realized that (amateur) copying of music was actually promoting sales. However, in the case of Napster, CD sales were down significantly. It is an open question whether copying or poor music quality was more responsible. Music commentators mention that currently industry producers have strong incentives to promote mediocre music in familiar genres. An accompanying issue is control of channels of distribution to allow such a strategy to succeed.[7] The compromise, centralized paid downloading, while convenient, is not the radical change Napster pioneered. I will hazard the prediction that Napster's technology may yet have another amazing application.

As the case of Napster shows, we can see clearly the facts about the IT situation—yet the ethical principles aren't clear. We see clearly that people can make digital copies at will, and that these copies are available to anyone on a large network. The ethical question is whether this is merely an extension of friends swapping copies (perfectly ethical) or whether it is an illegal (and unethical) violation of copyright. An entirely new method of sharing copies seems to require a rethinking of ethical principles. These issues are discussed more fully in Chapter IX, Copyright and Ownership.

Even when the circumstances are novel but the ethical principles are the same, working out the details may require more knowledge of IT than the average person has, and clearly such issues deserve to be discussed here. Although the ethical concepts of fraud and deceit may be familiar, their application in online contexts may not be familiar at all.

Therefore, an adequate discussion of the ethical issues involved in IT will require both a broad view of ethics and a sensitivity to the distinctive shifts it causes in our actions themselves. It is especially important that our views in ethics not be tied to familiar cases; we need to look beyond them to more general principles and theories to get the flexibility we need for an adequate discussion of the less familiar ethical issues raised by IT.[8] This is the aim of Chapter II, A Background in Ethical Theory.

Determining Right and Wrong

There is one more issue that needs to be addressed before we can begin surveying the actual problems of ethics and IT. The next question is: *Who is to say what is right and wrong?*

Even from the discussion so far, it should be clear that I think it is worthwhile to attempt to find the best answer we can to ethical questions. The obvious fact that there is disagreement about ethical questions no more shows that it is pointless to try to determine the best answer to ethical questions than disagreement about scientific issues would show it is pointless to try to resolve scientific disagreements. Disagreement about scientific issues can also be severe and can also last a long time. In the case of ethical issues, however, there is good evidence that there actually has been progress. Some practices condoned in the United States less than 200 years ago, such as slavery, are now regarded as outrageous.[9] So consensus can develop over time on the answers to ethical questions.

My view of ethics as higher level principles settling conflicts of interest can provide a basis for saying what is right and wrong. Ethical principles themselves can conflict, and it requires higher level principles to settle those conflicts. Some principles are clearly higher level than others. The social psychologist Lawrence Kohlberg, who was a pioneer in this area, developed a theory of different levels of ethical principles. Kohlberg (1976) believed that ethical reasoning develops in stages in human beings. People move to a different stage—and higher level of principle—precisely because they encounter irresolvable conflicts of principles at lower levels.[10]

Kohlberg's stages are:

- **Stage One:** Punishment and obedience
- **Stage Two:** Interests of only oneself
- **Stage Three:** Conformity for social approval
- **Stage Four:** Law and order
- **Stage Five:** Social contract based on utility
- **Stage Six:** Universal principles

Kohlberg thinks of children as moving through these stages. A person's development can stop at various stages. Children begin by obeying those in authority, usually parents, and are motivated to do so by the threat of punishment. Eventually, the child realizes that his own needs are not always satisfied by obedience, so his motivation changes; that is, he obeys when it satisfies his own needs, and may not obey when his needs come into conflict with parental demands. Those who never get beyond Stage Two, acting only on what they perceive satisfies only their needs, often spend large periods of time incarcerated. The major impetus for advancing to the next stage is conflicts that cannot be resolved at the stage below. Thus, the Stage Two sociopath must recognize social norms that come before self interest in order to do at all well in the social context in which his needs have to be met.

But individuals at Stage Three (Conformity) are motivated primarily by considerations of "looking good" in the eyes of others, and a person may find it impossible to be all things to all people. A common teenage conflict is between peer approval and the approval of older authorities such as parents, and…"who is to say who is right?" Obviously, neither. We need to move beyond social approval as the basis for ethical judgments.[11] Instead, we look to the social order, to laws and duties prescribed by society. This is Stage Four (Law and Order); now we obey to preserve social harmony.

As we consider the different stages, one can recognize people who simply stop at a given stage. Those who stop at Stage Three (Conformity) are very shallow people and, unless protected by others, will probably never have really fulfilling lives. Those who stop at Stage Four (Law and Order) are often quite functional. The reason why Stage Four is not the end of the line is, again, that laws and duties prescribed by society can conflict, either within themselves or across different societies or social groups, or with other values. The question then is where do these laws and duties get their authority? The Stage Four answer is "They just are what they are, period." Stage Four responses occur with some frequency in letters to the editor that point out that illegal immigration or medical marijuana are illegal and regard this observation as the final word in the discussion.

The Stage Five (Social Contract) answer goes beyond this. Kohlberg's Stage Five, which he thinks is embodied in the U.S. Constitution and its government, derives the authority of the law and social duties from the consent of the governed There is a social contract, and laws and duties can be changed to maximize social utility, "the greatest good for the greatest number." In certain circumstances, it can even be justified to break a law to demonstrate a higher principle (this is called civil disobedience).

Stage Five (Social Contract) itself is not without conflict. Doing the greatest good for the greatest number may not actually produce the best result. For example, enslaving 10% of the population may produce greater overall economic benefits but could no longer be accepted as a just social organization. If we generalize on Stage Five, we arrive at a more abstract social contract, in which principles are chosen that best express us as free and equal rational beings living together in a society, as in the U.S. Declaration of Independence and Constitution.

The principles arrived at in the various stages are discussed in traditional ethical theory. (A synopsis is included in the next chapter.) A major advantage of Kohlberg's staged approach is that it makes clear the reasons for the priority of some principles over others, and thus a basis for answering the question, who is to say what is right and wrong? The answer is: "The person with the most overall view using the highest level principles."[12] And a principle is not higher level because someone says it is, but because, in fact, it can settle conflicts irresolvable by lower level principles.

Indeed, ethical relativism, the view that all ethical views are equally good, is a Stage Two (Interests of self) view in Kohlberg's model, and in that view, social cooperation is either fragile or impossible. Since this is not true of human beings—we can and must cooperate since, as social animals, most of us could not survive outside society—ethical relativism is only possible as the view of a small minority. Hence, it can hardly be a universal high-level principle. There will be more on this issue in the next chapter, A Background in Ethical Theory.

For those without much background in philosophical ethics, the following chapter may be intimidating. I would encourage you first just to get an overall idea of what is in the chapter. Much of the discussion in the chapters following, especially applications of Rawls' theory of justice, depends on material from Chapter II. However, you can come back to Chapter II later on, on an as-needed basis. For those who already have some background in philosophical ethics, you may meet some old friends in a new setting. The very unpredictability of ethical problems of IT makes philosophical ethics even more relevant. Cut-and-dried solutions no longer apply, and only a more theoretical approach with deeper principles can give us the flexibility to deal with our new ethical environment.

References

Ante, S. E. (2004). Shifting work offshore? Outsourcer beware. *Business Week*, January 12.

Aristotle (350 BCE). *Nicomachean ethics*. Retrieved on May 10, 2004, from http://classics.mit.edu/Aristotle/nicomachaen.html

Gilligan, C. (1982). *In a different voice*. Cambridge, MA: Harvard University Press.

Johnson, D. (1985). *Computer ethics*. Englewood Cliffs, NJ: Prentice-Hall.

Kohlberg, L. (1976). Moral stages and moralization. In T. Lickona (Ed.), *Moral development and behavior* (pp. 31-53). New York: Holt, Rinehart & Winston.

Rawls, J. (1999). *A theory of justice,* (rev.ed.). Cambridge, MA: Harvard University Press.

Reynolds, G. (2003). *Ethics in information technology*. Boston, MA: Course Technology.

Tavani, H. (2003). *Ethics and technology*. Hoboken, NJ: Wiley.

Ziff, P. (1960). *Semantic analysis*. Ithaca, NY: Cornell University Press.

Endnotes

1   See Johnson (1985), an earlier example of a text on computer ethics; and Reynolds (2003) for a recent example. The range of issues is similar, and the primary focus of both is issues of professional ethics and privacy and security. Tavani (2003) adds a few chapters on social issues, but many of the main issues of this book are not addressed.

2   Gregory Mankiw, chair of White House Council of Economic Advisers, February 2004.

3   The question of the ethical status of corporations is also discussed extensively in Chapter X, Copyright and Ownership.

4   See Chapters V, VI, VII, VIII, IX, and X.

5   These issues are discussed at greater length in Chapter VII, Offshoring as an Ethical Issue.

6   Similar versions of this definition of value appear in Aristotle (350 BCE), Ziff (1960), and Rawls (1999).

7   My thanks to Neil Anapol for this point.

8   I am indebted to Douglas Cremer for this point.

9   Current attempts to prohibit same-sex marriage by constitutional amendment may end up the same way. Certainly very few would now approve of the early 20th Century attempts to pass a constitutional amendment to prohibit interracial marriage.

10   Social psychologist Carol Gilligan (1982) claims that Kohlberg's stages apply primarily to men. Since she also at one point claimed that women were much more likely to take a "correct" moral perspective, it is difficult to know how much weight to give to her claims. See Gilligan 1982.

11   Character-based Greek ethics, and the ethics of reputation, are at this stage. We don't necessarily leave such earlier stages behind; rather, we add higher level considerations.

12   This is a restatement of one of Steve Markoff's principles, "The highest value has the most overall view."

Chapter II

A Background in Ethical Theory

In this book, "ethics" is a general term for concerns about what people should do. The term "ethics" comes from the Greek word *ethike,* which means "character." Indeed, the ancient Greeks conceived issues about what people should do in terms of impact upon character—whether people were of good or bad character (Aristotle, 350 BCE). Our concern with good reputation reveals this kind of thinking, but bad actions and bad performance can be more important than any amount of good reputation if they are bad enough. Not even the most capable network troubleshooter could survive the discovery of large amounts of downloaded kiddie porn on his workstation.

William Bennett's *A Book of Virtues* (Bennett, 1993) is a more recent example of a character-based ethics very similar to Greek ethics. The central term of Greek ethics, *ethike arête,* is usually translated as "virtue"—the literal meaning is "excellence of character." "Good character traits" is probably the nearest translation. Bennett's list of virtues or good character traits includes: self-discipline, compassion, responsibility, friendship, work, courage, persever-ance, honesty, loyalty, and faith. His selection of virtues overlaps with the classic Greek virtues or good character traits. Plato's list was: courage, temperance, wisdom, and justice. (Plato, 360 BCE). Aristotle added liberality, pride, good temper, friendliness, truthfulness, and ready wit. Although all of these—Plato's, Aristotle's, and Bennett's—are good character traits to have, having them doesn't answer many important questions about what actions to do, especially when virtues conflict. Is perseverance in constructing a computer virus a good thing? Clearly the rightness or wrongness of the action in which we are persevering is very important. Or what about loyalty to an organization ripping off poor people? Here honesty (and compassion) may be more important than loyalty and responsibility. Indeed, Bennett's list omits justice, considered the most important virtue by Plato. Since justice is primarily a virtue of institutions rather than individuals, Bennett's list leaves out issues about how well society is arranged. We have made some progress on these issues since Greek times.[1]

The point is that character-based ethics is incomplete. Bennett himself, in replying to critics of his compulsive gambling behavior, seems to believe that as long as an individual has the "virtues," that is, the good character traits, then other actions are irrelevant. Most of the rest of us in these non-classic-Greek times believe otherwise. Nowadays, "ethics" is an inclusive term for concerns also referred to as "morality," "value," and "justice." Besides character, ethics in this inclusive sense is also concerned with the rightness and wrongness of actions, the value or goodness of things and situations, and with the justness of institutions. The basic terms of ethics are: right, good, and just.

Right, Good, Just

Although the Greek emphasis on character as the basis of ethics has not disappeared, our emphasis is much more upon action. We believe that some actions are right or wrong regardless of their impact on character. Child pornography is an extreme example. Less extreme but more important every-day examples include keeping a promise or other agreement and fulfilling a contract. What we now call *professional ethics* concerns itself almost entirely with what actions are right or wrong for a professional to do. Thus, an IT professional is called upon to deliver on contracts on time and to protect the proprietary information of his employer or client. The focus moves from character to action and from good or bad character to right or wrong action. So in addition to an explanation of what constitutes good or bad character, contemporary ethics must also provide an explanation of what makes actions right or wrong.

Along with the rightness and wrongness of actions, concerns about what we should do are greatly influenced by considerations of value. We (and the ancient Greeks) also need a *theory of value*, an explanation of why some things are good and others are not. Indeed, a very plausible theory of right is that the right thing to do is what produces the greatest good for the greatest number. This theory is called *utilitarianism* (Mill, 1863). [2]

The other important term included in ethics is revealed by the consideration that people, for example, the employees of a firm or the citizens of a state, can be of good character and do the right thing and yet keep in motion *institutions* of great evil. Thus, the morality of institutions needs to be assessed as well. This insight comes not only through our experience with genocide in the 20th century, but has been available since classic Greek times. Plato, for example, even thought that ethics for the individual was actually derived from the correct order of institutions in a society (Plato, 350 BCE). In recent times, we still see the need to assess whether institutions are just or unjust. So we need an explanation of how to determine the justice or injustice of institutions.

Justice, goodness, and *rightness* are thus the key areas of ethics.

The Rational Basis of Ethics

When I raised the question of "who is to say what is right and wrong?" in Chapter I, the answer was "The person with the most overall view using the highest level principles."[3] A principle is not higher level because someone says it is, but rather because, in fact, it can settle conflicts irresolvable by lower level principles. Indeed, ethical relativism, the view that all ethical views are equally good, is a view that makes social cooperation either fragile or impossible. Since, as social animals, most of us could not survive without social cooperation, ethical relativism is only possible as very much a minority view. Therefore, it can hardly be a universal high-level principle.

These considerations are the basis for a rational foundation for ethics. We find that we have conflicting principles of action and that there are higher level principles that can resolve these conflicts only if we treat them as overriding the lower level principles. For example, considerations of self-interest are trumped by principles yielding cooperative benefits only if most everyone follows them. To get the benefits of agreements, everyone must agree to keep agreements, at least most of the time, even when they could do better for themselves otherwise.

It is important to see the nature of the conflict between interests and higher level ethical principles. It can always look as though one can do better by not being ethical, and thus that ethics demands a departure from rationality. The situation is discussed in Game Theory, the theory of rational choices. The name of the type of choice situation is the Prisoner's Dilemma. The classic story that gives it that name is this: A prosecutor is sure that two prisoners are guilty, but does not have enough evidence to convict them. He offers each of them (separately) a deal: If neither confesses, they will receive medium sentences. If both confess, they will receive light sentences. If one prisoner confesses, he will be treated more leniently than in any other case, but the non-confessing prisoner will receive a maximum sentence (Luce & Raiffa, 1957). The situation can be represented as a *payoff matrix* (see Figure 1).

The pairs of numbers give Prisoner A's and then Prisoner B's ranking of the outcome. Thus, if Prisoner A confesses and Prisoner B does not, Prisoner A gets his first choice outcome (most lenient sentence) and Prisoner B gets his worst choice outcome (maximum sentence).

The payoff matrix applies unchanged to most situations in which there is a higher level ethical principle providing cooperative benefits, and the choice is to observe that principle or not to observe and act on self-interest instead (see Figure 2)[4].

What the payoff matrix reflects is that one can always do better from a selfish or self-interested point of view if everyone else obeys the (cooperative ethical) principle but you do not. For example, obeying traffic signals. If I obey, I may have to wait extra time. But if I am thinking in a purely self-interested (selfish) manner, I may go through the red light when it looks safe to me. I am attempting to avoid whatever disadvantage or burden there is for obeying and, at the same

Figure 1.

	Prisoner A confesses	Prisoner A does not confess
Prisoner B confesses	(2,2)	(4,1)
Prisoner B does not confess	(1,4)	(3,3)

Figure 2.

	Person A obeys principle	Person A disobeys (acts selfishly)
Person B obeys principle	(2,2)	(4,1)
Person B disobeys (acts selfishly)	(1,4)	(3,3)

time, get the benefit of the cooperative principle. Of course, the rub is that if everyone acts this way, the cooperative principle with its cooperative benefits is no longer available—we are at alternative (3,3), which means everyone is *collectively* worse off than if everyone obeyed (2,2). Therefore, the only way we can have ethical principles is if we treat principles that are cooperatively rational (produce 2,2 as opposed to 3,3) as a higher priority than considerations of self-interest (Schultz, 1971). A more extreme but perhaps more compelling example is that we agree not to use deadly force against each other and relegate the use of deadly force to a sovereign. The philosopher Hobbes (1651) thought this agreement was the essential social contract that removes us from a state of nature, described by Hobbes as a "war of all against all," guaranteeing that our lives will be "solitary, poore, nasty, brutish and short" (Hobbes, 1651, Ch. XIII).

People taking advantage of cooperative schemes are called "free riders." Although enforceable penalties help with free riders and may sometimes be necessary, they reduce cooperative benefits. And, in general, people expect to obey ethical principles even though there may be no obvious or immediate penalties.

The reasoning involved in giving principles yielding cooperative benefit higher priority than self-interest can be applied at higher levels: Whenever principles conflict for a type of action, there is the possibility of higher level principles resolving the conflict in a way that adds value. Thus, there is the possibility of higher level principles for the behavior of nations that add value if they are treated as higher level. Without such principles, we are left with wars, which are rarely in any society's interest.

The rational basis for ethics is thus the principle of higher level principles. It states that, other things being equal, it is rational to follow a higher level principle when that principle needs to be treated that way in order to resolve conflicts between lower level principles (Schultz, 1971). "Other things being equal" includes the reasonableness of other principles already being followed and the likelihood of the principle being publicly adopted. The task of ethics, so conceived, is to discover, formulate, and promulgate such a system of principles. It is a task we human beings began at least 2500 years ago, and we have made some progress. As we rapidly expand the scope of our powers of action through technology and information technology, one can hope that our progress in our ability to understand how to use these powers in the highest and best ways will keep pace.

Theories of Right: Intuitionist vs. End-Based vs. Duty-Based

So what makes an action right? There are three kinds of theories of right action: intuitionist, end-based, and duty-based. The first theory of right, intuitionism, is actually a non-theory. It says that there is no good explanation of right and wrong. Nevertheless, we have strong intuitive feelings about what is right and wrong that need no justification. The Ten Commandments, taken on their own, are an intuitionist theory. Two major difficulties with intuitionism are, first, that it is very unsatisfying just to be told that certain actions are right or wrong with no further justification. Second, when different kinds of right action conflict, we have no way of deciding priorities. If we are told: Honor thy father and mother, and also told: Do not steal, then what do we do if our father orders us to steal? For example, in an episode of the TV show *The Simpsons* dealing with the Ten Commandments, Homer (the father) has stolen cable TV access. His daughter Lisa's spiritual advisor reminds her that to turn her father in would violate the commandment to honor thy father and mother (Pepoon, 1991). The answer may be obvious to us that the command "Do not steal" has precedence, but if so, we are using something in addition to an intuitive list of wrong actions to decide.

End-based theories of right action simplify things by reducing considerations of right action to considerations of pursuing some end, usually goodness. A very common formula, *utilitarianism,* has much plausibility: Act so as to produce the greatest amount of good for the greatest number (Utilitarian Principle). For how could it possibly be wrong to do the action that produces the greatest good? How could it possibly be right to do an action that produces less good when you could have done better?

Although a plausible idea, utilitarianism suffers from two major difficulties. One is that if we consider actions in isolation from one another, it is easy for a utilitarian to break promises or fail to fulfill contracts when more good would be produced in that case. Breaking copy protection to give software to a needy organization doing good for homeless people seems acceptable on utilitarian grounds. The trouble is that then institutions that allow us to cooperate, to live and work together, would disintegrate. If, in individual cases, breaking copy protection may produce more good, we cannot realize the overall good of not allowing copying and thus providing an environment for software development. Thus, important goods are not available unless we consider ourselves bound to follow certain rules. Considerations like these are important in the discussion of copyright and piracy in Chapter IX.

But utilitarianism can achieve these goods if it is considered as a theory of just institutions rather than individual acts. Then, one is still bound by social rules governing the institutions of keeping agreements and fulfilling contracts even though more good might be done in the individual case by breaking the social rule. One does actions not because the individual actions produce the greatest amount of good, but because the right action is to follow social rules that produce the greatest amount of good. This theory is called *rule utilitarianism*.

But how do we tell which rules these are? The second major difficulty is that summing goodness over individuals in any reasonable way has proved to be impossible. Therefore, the notion of the greatest good for the greatest number can only serve as a metaphor. It simply can't be made usably precise (Arrow, 1951).[5]

The major alternative to end-based theories of right action is a duty-based theory. Duty-based theories insist that rightness is independent of goodness. Perhaps the most developed duty-based theory is due to the philosopher Immanuel Kant, founded on his *Categorical Imperative* (Kant, 1785). Following the Categorical Imperative, one acts on principles that could be willed to be universal law. For example, making an agreement you have no intention of keeping could not be willed to be universal law because then no one would make agreements. The biblical Golden Rule, do unto others as you would have them do unto you, is a similar but less formal version of Kant's principle.

There are a number of superficial criticisms of Kant's principle, mainly about technicalities in its wording and application. It is important in Kant's theory that what is judged for rightness or wrongness is your action together with its motive. The test of rightness is whether your action *as done from that motive* could be made a universal principle of action (Nell, 1975). Therefore, Kant's principle, correctly understood, does not allow "tailoring" the action to the circumstances. For example, "I will fail to keep agreements only to people without the resources to sue," when your agreement is with people without the resources to sue, is not a legitimate application of Kant's principle. (Insurance companies would, therefore, sometimes be in violation of Kant's principle.)

Kant's principle would handle the previous case of breaking copy protection to give software to a needy organization doing good for homeless people by a careful (self-) examination of motives. Is my principle to do good in a particular case regardless of the social rules? Everyone's acting on that principle will result in there being no rules and thus no software and thus no opportunity to break copy protection. This cannot be a right action with that motive. However, if my principle is to break the social rule only in cases where great harm would otherwise occur, this could be a right action. For example, breaking an encryption to obtain medical information needed immediately to save someone's life would clearly be the right thing to do. The tricky thing is to estimate the relative consequences. It is important to consider actual social rules, and there is clearly a presumption that they are not to be broken lightly.

Frequently, the consideration of *publicity* can provide guidance in using Kant's principle. *Publicity* requires that everyone concerned be aware of the principle you are using. This immediately rules out exceptions to principles that can't be publicized because those not granted the exception would know they had been unjustly treated. For example, a student does not satisfy a requirement for graduation but is granted a diploma on the condition that he is not to tell anyone that the exemption was made. Kant's principle is clearly not satisfied.

Kant has little guidance for what to do when right actions conflict, except to say that the stronger ground of obligation has precedence (Kant, 1797b). However, he doesn't give directions on how to determine this. Therefore, in this respect, Kant's theory of right action is incomplete and needs the addition of a theory of just social rules, especially how they fit together into a system without conflicts. Kant has such a theory in his *Metaphysical Elements of Justice* (Kant, 1797a), but rather than discuss Kant's theory of justice, I will use a modern update by the 20th century philosopher, John Rawls (Rawls, 1999a).

Both rule utilitarianism and Kant's principle offer similar and often identical answers to the questions of right and wrong, but there are cases in which they differ. If there are grounds for deciding between them, it lies in the nature of the contribution each makes to a theory of justice, of what systems of social rules deserve our obedience. We will return to the question of justice shortly.

Some think that the attempt to reduce ethics to rational calculation is misguided. The 18th century philosopher, David Hume, for example, thought that ethics would not be possible without feelings of sympathy of one human being for another (Hume, 1739, 1751). Without these feelings, it would not be possible for us to include others within the sphere of our own interests.[6] The claim is that formal ethical theories, especially Kant's, ignore the importance of moral feeling. We are inclined to help other people not because we see that the principles of our action could be willed to be universal law, but because we feel for other people's predicaments and are moved to help them (Baier, 1992, pp.56-58).

Kant (1797b, pp.451-453) does derive the duty of mutual aid from his principle. A principle of not helping others when they are in need could not be universal law because one would want such aid oneself when one was in need. Although this seems cold and unfeeling, Kant also discusses the role of feeling. Although moral feelings such as sympathy are important and need to be cultivated, they can't be the ground for the rightness of the action. Otherwise, one could avoid helping other people on the grounds that one simply didn't feel like it. One is probably a better person (good character again) if one has a robust set of moral feelings that help one make the correct ethical decisions and help one carry through one's ethical decisions. But such feelings are not the basis of rightness or goodness or justice. The feelings follow from rightness, goodness, and justice as determined by rational principles.

Rights, Duties, Obligations

Several other common ethical terms can be defined starting from right and wrong action. *Duties* and *obligations* are actions it would be *wrong* not to do. *Duties* come about just from the nature of the situation one is in, for example, being a parent. Whereas *obligations* come about because of something one has done to obligate oneself, for example, sign a contract or accept a benefit. A person has a *right* to do something or have something when it would be *wrong* to prevent him from doing the action or having the object.

Duties and obligations have different characteristics. Normally, obligations require one to do a specific action or set of actions. For example, if I have an obligation to correct the faults in my installation of your network, then that is the action I am ethically required to do. But if I have a duty as an IT professional to help underfunded educational facilities, it is, to a large extent, my choice which educational facilities I help. I obvious am not ethically required to help *all* educational facilities. I cannot be required to help them all because my cost would be too great.[7] This is very often the limiting proviso on duties—the actions mentioned in a duty are required only if the cost to oneself is not too great[8] (Kant 1797b, p.392).

Because each of these ethical items can easily conflict, they should always be regarded as derived from an acceptable theory of right and wrong action. It is not uncommon for people to think that, because they have a right to do something, that is the end of the story, ethically speaking. Whereas a right—which is based on reasons for not preventing a person from doing an action—may have to be weighed against reasons for not preventing other people from doing conflicting actions. I may have a right to buy a competing software company, but that right may be outweighed by society's right to prevent monopolies. It is clearer to work in terms of right and wrong than rights. If society does have a right to prevent monopolies, one needs to recognize that the operative ethical principle is that it is wrong to create monopolies and that individual rights to acquire property can be superseded.[9]

Theory of Value

In a way, it is too bad that it is so difficult to make utilitarianism a practical guide to right action, because then two of the key ethical concepts—rightness and justice—would be reduced in a relatively simple way to goodness. And goodness or value is easier to explain.

To understand goodness, we must look to interests considered from a point of view. A good or valuable object is one that, to a greater degree than average, answers to the interests one has in the object from a certain point of view.[10] Thus, a good disk drive is one that answers to the interests of a computer user in safely storing information. Very often, the objects that we deal with are actually defined in terms of functions, and then the value of that object simply consists in its performing that function to a greater degree than average; that is, good antivirus software must prevent and destroy viruses, a good keyboard cleaner must clean keyboards well, and so on.

Very often, we simply assume that the point of view from which value is to be evaluated is our own or that of our group. Most disagreements about value are, in fact, disagreements about the appropriate point of view to use for evaluation. But within a point of view, there is nothing especially subjective about value. Whether something is valuable from a point of view is a matter of fact.

One especially important set of values are *enabling* values, for example, health, education, and wealth. We must have these things to a certain level if we are going to be able to pursue any interests at all.[11] They need not lead to the fulfillment of some particular ends or realization of some particular function. These enabling values are especially important in considering the justice of social arrangements, because if people are unable to have them, their ability to live satisfactory lives is greatly reduced. They thus provide a basic measure of whether people are better or worse off. In the social contract theory of justice we will next consider, enabling values play a critical role.

Conflicting Principles and Priorities

Ethical problems first arise because there are conflicts between different interests that cannot be resolved on the level of interests alone. Higher level principles need to be applied. We have seen that the role of ethical principles of various levels is to resolve conflicts between lower level principles that cannot be resolved on the same level as the conflicting principles.

Thus, individuals have their own interests. There might actually be no need for ethics if everyone could get everything they wanted without conflict with other people. But we live in a world (and in societies) in which this is not true. There are conflicts of interest. These need to be resolved in a fair way. It is also to everyone's advantage to have procedures for handling recurring conflicts that people accept. This gives rise to principles involving negotiated agreements and keeping them. Enough people see that reasons for keeping cooperative agreement have to be given higher priority than reasons of individual interest for these principles to operate at all.

Actually, it is probably incorrect even to think that human beings have any alternative but to live in society. Human beings have evolved as social animals, and this means it is difficult or impossible for them to survive outside of a society. However, there are still questions about the constitution of societies. Individuals can sometimes join a different society or consider alternative arrangements of social rules for their own society. But, just as all individuals can't get everything they want, no one set of social rules satisfies everyone's interests perfectly. The question is how to handle cases in which generally beneficial social rules are worse than they could be for some members of a society.

There are two conflicting considerations in these cases. First, the fact that there is a grievance against the social rules isn't enough by itself to release people from the obligation to obey the rules. The individual can't *directly* opt out of social rules. (Although in extreme circumstances they can; for example, if the society is killing its own members, most obligations to follow the rules are void.) And, second, ultimately a just society is for the individual, so ultimately the individuals in the society have the right (and sometimes the obligation) to decide that some rules should no longer to be followed. John Locke (1690), the strongest influence on the founding fathers of the United States, put this point very strongly: "Who shall be judge whether [government] act contrary to their trust?...The people shall be judge" (Chapter XIX).

Once again, if this conflict is going to be resolved in an ethical way, there must be higher level principles to which to appeal. In the case of a constitutional democracy, higher level appeals can be directed to the electorate, through changing legislators or through initiatives, or to the constitution through the court system. But it certainly has been the experience in constitutional democracies and in the United States that the constitution itself has been flawed and requires revision, or that the electorate itself is unresponsive. The prime example is slavery and the ensuing treatment of African-Americans. The principles appealed to in cases where the regular institutional paths have failed to address the issue are the principles of justice behind the constitution.

In cases of civil disobedience, perhaps most clearly in the United States as practiced by Martin Luther King, Jr., the law is broken not on the grounds that the lawbreakers now have the right to break any law or even particular laws, but rather to address the sense of justice, the commitment of the people to the principles underlying the laws (King, 1963). It should be noted again, that although majority rule is a good choice of procedure to make a group decision, it by no means guarantees a reasonable or fair decision, and there is no reason to change one's beliefs just because of what the majority thinks.[12] There are actually built-in guarantees that systems of social rules won't work perfectly.

Also, if it is decided that the constitution needs to be revised, the appeal has to be to principles above and beyond the constitution, so once again we need to appeal to principles deciding what institutions and social arrangements are truly just and which are not. We now turn to the principles of justice.

A Theory of Justice

To determine the justice of institutions and systems of social rules, we also need to draw on the concepts of right, wrong, and value. Assessments of justice are based on our individual ideas of right and wrong and assume that we are able to assess values more-or-less correctly. The theory of justice of this book is John Rawls' elaboration of the social contract theory underlying the society of the United States (Rawls, 1999a). The basic idea of a social contract is that a justly ordered society is one to which individuals can freely decide to obligate themselves.[13] This idea is clearly expressed by the Declaration of Independence of the United States of 1776.

But if we take this idea seriously, our decision will very likely be biased if we base it on our current situation. Hence, Rawls' major addition is to say that the decision must be made prior to being in society, without knowledge of what our position will be in society, and it will be a decision we will be obligated to stick to and expect others to make and stick to as well. Rawls calls this decision about the basic principles of society the *original position.* It is never actually a position we are in, because we are all born into some society or other, yet it is a position we can return to in order to evaluate our institutions.[14]

So, what principles would be chosen? Rule utilitarianism is a plausible candidate, that is, act on the set of rules likely to produce the greatest amount of good for the greatest number. But what if in society you end up as a slave? A rule-utilitarian, 19th-century, Southern plantation owner could (and did) feel fine with a system producing perhaps the greatest good for the greatest number, even if it did require some to be deprived of basic liberties. In this respect, the Declaration of Independence and the Bill of Rights of the U.S. Constitution are non-rule utilitarian. They insist that each individual has basic liberties that are not to be compromised or traded off for other benefits. Rawls (1999a) calls this the First Principle of Justice or the Greatest Equal Liberty; that is, society is to be arranged so that all members have the greatest equal liberty possible for all, including fair equality of opportunity.

For Americans, there should be no argument that this principle would be chosen above all others to govern society's arrangements. In addition to the basic freedoms, such as freedom of speech, assembly, religion, and so on, it includes equality of opportunity. Thus, society's rules are not biased against anyone in it and allow all to pursue their interests and realize their abilities.[15]

The Second Principle of Justice Rawls (1999a) calls the Difference Principle: economic inequalities in society are justified insofar as they make members of the least advantaged social class, better off than if there were no inequality. "Better off" is to be measured against enabling values affected by the social structure that reflect an individual's life prospects. Rawls (1999a, p.78) cites authority, income, and wealth as those enabling values.

Rawls (1999a) also indicates we should apply the Difference Principle to the background institutions, the major institutions that determine people's life prospects. Certainly, a market economy, especially with respect to employment, could be part of this background structure. When applying the Difference Principle, we consider the effects of the background structure on the life prospects of representatives from each relevant socioeconomic class—for example laborers, white-collar workers, managers, employers, corporate officers, investors, and so on. Then, of the efficient background structures favoring one class over another, choose the one that makes the worst-off class best off (Rawls 1999a, sections 2, 16). The social contract basis for this principle is straightforward: If you are entering a society with no knowledge of your specific place in that society, the Difference Principle guarantees that you will be no worse off than you need be to keep the society functioning.

Rawls (2001) indicated at one time that the second principle could be replaced by Rule Utilitarianism, with a minimum; in other words, not any economic distribution would be allowed, but only those with an acceptable minimum.[16] So, in an oversimplified example, giving slaves their freedom would be an advance in the justness of society—a serious violation of the Greatest Equal Freedom Principle would be corrected. But if the slaves are kept in the same, or worse, economic situation, then the Difference Principle may be violated. We can understand ongoing debates in terms of these principles. Affirmative action, for example, can be seen both as a violation of the basic freedoms of some (those denied admission in order to allow minorities to attend law school, for example) or an attempt to create fair equality of opportunity for others (minorities denied good public education are given compensatory treatment). Even though there is bitter disagreement, one can see how both sides of this debate can be framed in terms of the two principles of justice.

The same is true for the range of social and ethical issues of IT. Discussions about offshoring often justify the practice in terms of benefits for all. But as we have seen, the contention that all will benefit is hardly the end of the ethical discussion. Even leaving aside the difficulty in establishing this contention, there are still issues about what society we are considering. At this point, for all the talk of a global economy, we don't have anything like a global society with free and equal competitors in that economy. There are consequences for ethical behavior in this situation.

A market economy is a very good candidate to be a background institution in a society obeying the Difference Principle. A market economy's efficiency— no one is able to be better off without someone else being worse off—goes a long way toward satisfying the Difference Principle. Efficiency in a market economy means that there is no slack. And no administrative overhead means that there are more resources to distribute. But efficiency is not all there is to the Difference Principle.

Economists and social theorists accept that justice (or equity) is more than efficiency.[17] In fact, as Rawls (1999a) points out, there can be many efficient distributions, even including absurd ones where someone has all the economic goods and everyone else has nothing. If Rupert Murdoch were to achieve this situation (he seems to be trying), it would be efficient—he would lose if any economic goods were transferred to anyone else. American society is not based upon a market economy as the primary ethical justification for social rules, even in economic matters. A market economy is a good candidate to be an institution in a just society because of its efficiency and its compatibility with the Principle of Greatest Equal Freedom. But without some social constraints, an unregulated market economy can allow monopolies, which have no competitive pressure to be efficient or to respond to the needs of customers or to price goods in a fair way. This issue is discussed in connection with Microsoft in Chapter V, Justice in a Market Economy.

There is a great deal of evidence that Rawls' Difference Principle is in fact accepted as a basis for the discussion of public policy by both conservatives and liberals in the United States (Rawls, 1999a). Liberal attempts to improve the lot of those worst off are usually challenged by conservatives on the basis that these attempts will make the worst off even less well off. Two examples: attempts to raise the minimum wage are challenged with the claim that employers will be able to hire less people; and attempts to require home developers to build a certain percentage of low-income housing are challenged on the grounds that developers will decide not to develop rather than cut their profits (Svorny, 2004). In both cases, the conservative argument is that proposals intended to make the worst off better off will instead make them still worse off. Regardless of whether these claims are true—and there is a big difference between whether we consider small businesses or multibillion-dollar corporations—both conservatives and liberals in these debates are clearly accepting the Difference Principle as a basis for discussion.

So there is a pretty good case that Rawls' two principles of justice are indeed the ones most Americans accept as higher level principles (Rawls, 1999a). Recall that most Americans are very unwilling to trade off freedom for economic or other benefits. Also, even defenders of offshoring don't simply defend it on the ground that it raises average utility; rather, the argument is that everyone will be better off. So I believe some version of the Difference Principle, making the worst off best off, is being appealed to.

But the principles of justice are sometimes not followed. Rawls (1993) made a critically important change to his original statement of the principles of justice during the 1980s. It is that in a constitutional democracy, such as the United States with freedom of opinion and religion, we can't expect agreement on what Rawls calls *comprehensive doctrines,* that is, doctrines about the ultimate nature of man, or even moral doctrines (Rawls, 1993, pp. 12-15). Such a society must be pluralistic in these matters. Consequently, attempts by religions to embed their own comprehensive doctrines in the constitution are a serious danger to a free society. For example, those proposing a constitutional amendment to prohibit gay marriage, presumably on religious grounds, are a serious a threat to the basis of American society.

I have made very little mention of religion as the basis for ethics (besides mentioning the Golden Rule). The difficulty is that, although religion has historically been the repository of much ethical knowledge, the ethical knowledge is usually thoroughly mixed with principles and commands that require commitment to special religious practices. For example, not going to Mass is not wrong for non-Catholics. In some cases, this can lead to a de-emphasis of important ethical principles in favor of principles more central to religious observances. Religion also can add sanctions such as going to Hell for unethical behavior, but these sanctions apply across the board to internal religious requirements and so are no special help to being ethical. Also, as we just saw above, fundamentalism can be a serious threat to a just society. So it is really an open question nowadays to what extent religion is an aid to ethical behavior. In the spirit of Rawls, a democratic pluralist society requires tolerance of all religions, but on the condition that those religions acknowledge that tolerance of other comprehensive doctrines is a condition of their being tolerated themselves (Rawls, 1999a, section 35).

There remain two further levels of principle because there are two further kinds of conflicts that ethics needs to address: one is conflict between societies; and the second is conflict between human needs and the environment. The ethical principles involved will be discussed in detail in later chapters: Principles concerning relations between societies will be discussed in Chapter VII, Offshoring as an Ethical Issue; and principles concerning human needs and the environment will be discussed in Part IV, Ultimate Questions. Here is a brief indication of what those additional principles look like.

In his later work *The Law of Peoples*, Rawls (1999b) considers how to extend the principles of justice to cover the international situation. His account has several distinctive features. First, a social contract view of international justice requires principles to be chosen, not by the political officials of each nation or nation state, but by *peoples*. On a social contract view, members of a given social group are the source of state and national authority, not the other way around. Rawls notes that this view differs from most discussions of international law since the 1600s.

Rawls (1999b) constructs a second social contract to govern relations between peoples. The principles chosen he calls the Law of Peoples. The basis for the second social contract is that the representatives of any society must be able to agree to principles without knowing how their society would be favored or disfavored by those principles. Once again, the agreement is fair, but this time it is between societies rather than individuals.

The principles that Rawls (1999b) claims would be chosen to regulate relations between societies are analogous to those principles that would be chosen by individuals to regulate their own societies. In priority order, they are:

1.   They honor human rights, respect each others freedom, and respect cooperative agreements made between them.

2.   Peoples do not intervene in each others affairs and only make war in self-defense. (These principles are analogous to the Greatest Equal Freedom Principle).

3.   Peoples have a duty to assist other people living under unfavorable conditions.[18] (This principle is analogous to the Difference Principle.)

Although the United States was a model for the Principles of Justice as a social contract of free and equal people within a particular society, it unfortunately fails as a model for the Law of Peoples as a social contract of free and equal societies. The United States has never endorsed the Universal Declaration of Human Rights (Chomsky, 1996). And, in the case of the recent war with Iraq, it has abandoned the principle of the Law of Peoples concerning war. If we accept the principles contained in the Law of Peoples as ethical principles, then war is justified only in self-defense. It follows that this war is unethical. It is grotesque to propose that destroying the infrastructure of a country, as in Iraq, has much to do with helping them. In any case, helping a country cannot be an excuse for violating the first two principles of respecting freedom and only making war in self-defense.

Finally, there are ethical principles concerning conflicts between human needs and the environment. Many of the relevant issues are discussed in Chapter XII, The Ultimate Value of Technology, and Chapter XIII, The Ultimate Value of information technology. There is again a choice of principles, and which are chosen depends on high-level beliefs about human technology and its relation to nature. If one believes that technology can correct its own errors in a timely manner and that a policy of unregulated technological progress is most conducive to overall human progress, then technological progress becomes the ultimate value and touchstone for policy. If one believes human technology has built-in unanticipated conflicts with the ecosystem, then what is called for is a policy of minimum mutilation of the ecosystem. The relevant point here is that the principles governing the overall utilization of technology, because of the far-reaching nature of that utilization, have to be on a higher level even than principles of justice and even those of principles of international justice.

References

Aristotle. (350 BCE). *Nicomachean ethics*. Retrieved on May 10, 2004, from http://classics.mit.edu/Aristotle/nicomachaen.html

Arrow, K. (1951). *Social choice and individual values*. New York: John Wiley & Sons.

Baier, A. (1992). *Moral prejudices*. Cambridge, MA: Harvard University Press.

Bennett, W. (1993). *A book of virtues*. New York: Simon & Schuster.

Chomsky, N. (1996). *Powers and prospects*. Boston, MA: South End Press.

Gauthier, D. (1967). Morality and advantage. *Philosophical Review, 27*, 460-475.

Hobbes, T. (1651). *Leviathan*. Retrieved on May 10, 2004, from http://darkwing.uoregon.edu/~rbear/hobbes/leviathan.html

Hume, D. (1739). *A treatise of human nature*. London: John Noon.

Hume, D. (1751). *An enquiry concerning the principles of morals*. Retrieved on August 7, 2005, from www.gutenberg.org/etext/4320

Kant, I. (1785). *Groundwork of the metaphysics of morals*. Retrieved on May 10, 2004, from http://www.swan.ac.uk/poli/texts/kant/kantcon.htm

Kant, I. (1797a). *Metaphysical elements of justice. Metaphysics of morals, Part I.* Konigsberg: Friedrich Nicolovius.

Kant, I. (1797b). *The doctrine of virtue. Metaphysics of morals, Part II.* Konigsberg: Friedrich Nicolovius.

King, M. L. Jr. (1963). Letter from Birmingham City Jail. *Liberation,* 10-16.

Locke, J. (1690). *The second treatise of government.* Retrieved on May 10, 2004, from http://www.constitution.org/jl/2ndtreat.htm

Luce, D. & Raiffa, H. (1967). *Games and decisions.* New York: John Wiley & Sons.

Mill, J. S. (1863). *Utilitarianism.* Retrieved on May 10, 2004, from *http://etext.library.adelaide.edu.au/m/mill/john_stuart/m645u/*

Nell (O'Neill), O. (1975). *Acting on principle.* New York: Columbia University Press.

Pepoon, S. (1991). *The Simpsons,* "Homer vs. Lisa and the 8th Commandment." Episode 7F13, Fox TV Network.

Plato. (360 BCE). *Republic.* Retrieved on May 10, 2004, from http://classics.mit.edu/Plato/republic.html

Rawls, J. (1993). *Political liberalism.* New York: Columbia University Press.

Rawls, J. (1999a). *A theory of justice* (rev. ed.). Cambridge, MA: Harvard University Press.

Rawls, J. (1999b). *The law of peoples.* Cambridge, MA: Harvard University Press.

Rawls, J. (2001). *Justice as fairness: A restatement.* Cambridge, MA: Harvard University Press.

Rousseau, J.-J. (1762). *The social contract.* Retrieved on May 10, 2004, from http://www.constitution.org/jjr/socon_01.htm

Schultz, R. (1971). Reasons to be moral. PhD Dissertation. Cambridge, MA: Harvard University.

Sen, A. (1961). *Collective choice and social welfare.* San Francisco: Holden-Day.

Svorny, S. (2004). Inclusionary zoning will not work. *San Fernando Valley Daily News*, April 4.

Ziff, P. (1960). *Semantic analysis.* Ithaca, NY: Cornell University Press.

Endnotes

1   For a similar criticism of Bennett's *Book of Virtues*, see http://www.kellysite.net/bennett.htm

2   Earlier versions were developed by David Hume and Jeremy Bentham.

3   This is a restatement of one of Steve Markoff's principles, "The highest value has the most overall view."

4   The application of the matrix to ethical principles is due to David Gauthier (1967), "Morality and Advantage."

5   Kenneth Arrow won the Nobel Prize in 1972 by proving in his "general possibility theorem" that a consistent and very minimally just amalgamation of individual preferences is impossible. Such an amalgamation is called a "social choice." Utilitarianism as a usable theory would need to make such impossible social choices. Arrow's proof uses fairly abstract mathematics (theory of partial orderings) and is not accessible to non-mathematicians. For a brief (but still technical) account, see encyclopedia.thefreedictionary.com/Arrow's+theorem.

6   Other philosophers, notably the Logical Positivists centered in Vienna until Nazism forced their dispersal, thought that this emotive content was all that there was to ethics. In effect, all ethical judgments are similar to cheers or boos: Murder, boo! Or Unselfishness, yea! This view would make it nonsensical to debate ethical issues, as people have done for several thousand years at least. So there would need to be a very good reason for holding this radical view, and there really isn't. The Logical Positivists generalized on a narrow view of science, which they took to be a standard of meaningfulness. For them, since ethical judgments didn't meet these narrow standards (direct verification by experience), they had to be explained some other way. However, theoretical scientific statements are rarely directly verifiable by experience. Also, the positivist standard of meaningfulness isn't verified by experience either. So on their own terms, the positivists were really saying, Verification, yea!

7   These distinctions follow those drawn by Rawls (1999a, Sections 18 and 19).

8   The cost would be too great if doing the action would interfere with your ability to fulfill your duties and obligations. That includes keeping up one's own well-being. For example, working for charitable organizations to such an extent that one's health is damaged would be too great a cost.

9   See Chapter V, Justice in a Market Economy.

10   Similar versions of this definition of value appear in Aristotle (350 BCE), Ziff (1960), and Rawls (1999a).

11   Rawls call these *primary goods*.

12   See Arrow (1951) and Sen (1961). The problem is that majority rule violates some minimal conditions on fair and reasonable group decisions. An even worse problem is that all procedures for group decisions violate the same minimal conditions. This result is called the Arrow Possibility Theorem. See also Endnote 5, this chapter.

13   Various influential early versions of social contract theory include Hobbes (1651), Locke (1690), and Rousseau (1762).

14   The original position is not unlike other positions in which our knowledge and interests are deliberately disregarded, for example, being a juror.

15   Rawls includes fair equality of opportunity under the second principle, but it seems to me to belong with the freedoms of the first principle which guarantee an unbiased starting place in society.

16   Rawls later feels that the "social minimum" cannot be clearly enough specified to provide a workable basis for assessing the justice of institutions, and, therefore, the Difference Principle without a minimum will yield better results (Rawls, 2001, 278-9). My own view is that the absence of a clear minimum will make the justification of the principles as reflecting a social contract much more difficult. Perhaps, as Rawls argues, the Difference Principle always does better for the least advantaged than principles including a minimum (Rawls, 2001, 61-65). But the considerations establishing this are so esoteric that their chances of being applied or understood in practice are not good.

17   This condition is known by economists as *Pareto optimality*. For Rawls' discussion of Pareto optimality and the Difference Principle, see Rawls (1999a, Sections 12 and 13).

18   In *Law of Peoples*, Rawls (1999b, pp. 35-38) states eight principles. "No World State" is not itself regarded as a principle, and I have condensed a few others. The one omission I find striking is agreement that there be a mechanism for dealing with violations of the principles.

Chapter III

The Context of IT Ethical Issues

A few other background issues deserve clarification before I examine specific ethical problems of information technology. IT always appears in the context of an organization, and so ethical problems of IT come to us with certain organizational interests attached. In this chapter, I note these interests and the points of view behind them. I also discuss in general terms the ethical problem of the individual who is required by an organization to do something he or she feels is unethical. This problem (and what can be done about it) is also part of the IT ethical context.

Within an Organization

In many cases within an organization, ethical considerations will be fairly clear—the ethical manager will execute his responsibilities to the best of his ability and the ethical employee will also do the same. The value to be maximized is the welfare of the organization, corporation, or business. If Joe White is employed to do technical support for the Anonymous Company, his ethical responsibilities as an employee will be determined by his job description and company policies, the background company culture, and the background social and legal institutions governing employment by a company. Typically, he will be required to be present at the job location for certain hours and during those hours provide technical support to specified employees, involving certain defined responsibilities and actions. If Mark Maxim is the CIO of Anonymous Company, he too has ethical responsibilities determined in the same way—by his job description and company policies, the background company culture, and the background social and legal institutions governing employment by a company. Typically, his responsibilities will be defined more generally, almost certainly including ensuring the continuing smooth functioning of IT in support of the goals of the organization. Relevant IT ethical issues can arise about the background justice of any of these determinants, that is, about documented company policies and procedures, the company culture, and the background social and legal institutions. These issues will be discussed in Chapter IV, Professional Duties, and Chapters V, VI, and VII, which consider the implications of the Principles of Justice on IT issues.

IT ethical issues within organizations also arise from the relation between IT professionals and non-IT personnel, who are also known as *users*. The questions are: How should users deal with IT professionals? How should IT professionals deal with the rest of the organization? And, how do we deal with issues stemming from the interaction of IT with the rest of the organization when such issues are not clearly the responsibility of either IT professionals or users? General management is responsible for answers to the last question.

Of course, the company culture and documented policies will be the first source to consult for answers to these questions. Here are areas where culture and/or policy are likely to set standards (Applegate, Austin, & McFarlan, 2003):

Users:
- Standards for responsiveness of IT staff to user operational needs
- User input into design, acquisition, and change of applications
- Appropriate user control of maintenance
- Information to users on IT changes
- Appropriate user contribution to data integrity

IT Professionals:
- Recognition and maintenance of IT professional standards
- Responsibility for hardware and software standards

- Professional control over application acquisition, including maintainability
- Responsibility for data integrity
- Standards for ongoing professional development

General Management (concerning the relationship of IT to the rest of the firm):

- Continuing assessment of IT value to the firm
- Monitoring overall fit of IT to organizational needs from both IT and non-IT points of view
- Standards for vendors
- Standards for user/IT relation and balance of power between the constituencies

To what extent do principles or standards in these areas raise ethical issues? For example, it is not in itself an ethical matter whether the integrity of the data is preserved. However, preserving data integrity is almost certainly essential to the survival of an organization. Therefore, preserving data integrity will be one of the duties of an ethical IT professional working for the organization. Because the ability to preserve data integrity is rooted in fairly technical considerations of database design, including normalization of tables, users and non-IT management may not appreciate why some constraints on the way data can be represented are necessary. For conflicts like these to be handled ethically, appropriate levels of responsibility and authority for IT (and all other) positions must be determined. Then it is up to the individual in that position to exercise his authority appropriately to fulfill his (ethical) responsibilities. The only ethical failure would be a failure to use authority appropriately to carry out one's responsibilities.

It is unfortunately not that uncommon to see mismatches between IT management and general management in a corporation. In fact, it is clearly a duty of top management to monitor the fit between IT and the rest of the organization to ensure that the most important overall interests of the company are preserved. It would also seem to be a duty for top management to acquire enough technical IT knowledge to understand the relevant management issues.

Some areas for IT professional standards exist because users may also lack relevant technical knowledge. Users are, to some extent, vulnerable because of their relative lack of technical expertise and clout. It is not that difficult for an unethical IT professional to take advantage of the situation, perhaps avoiding work by falsely claiming technical impossibility. There does seem to be a special duty on the part of IT professionals to take into account the diminished technical capacity of users and not take unfair advantage.

There is another connected user responsibility contained in the user issues cited above, namely, for users to have appropriate input into IT development and implementation. The ethical basis is that of users fulfilling their appropriate job responsibilities. However, users, by themselves, cannot have appropriate input unless the IT staff fulfills its duty to treat users properly by keeping them in the loop.

The duties of the IT staff itself are, to a large extent, the application of the general duties of the IT professional to the particular circumstances of the organization. The general duties of the IT professional are widely understood and accepted by IT professionals, and we will discuss their nature and justification in Chapter IV, Professional Duties. It is somewhat surprising that they are considerably broader than the duties of many other professions and even more surprising how generally these broader duties are acknowledged. In the IT professional areas mentioned above, hardware and software standards and application acquisition and maintainability are examples. IT professionals need to handle these areas, but they must consider the fit to the organization. Purely technical standards are not appropriate. And, although top management must monitor the goodness of fit of IT to company needs, goals, and strategies, IT staff must have appropriateness to the company in mind when acquiring applications; otherwise, there will not be much to monitor. Upper management, normally the CEO, is indeed responsible for an overall view of how well IT is functioning within the organization, but without an IT staff that is aware of its professional duties within the organization, it will not be easy for IT to function well.

Besides issues of the fit of IT to the rest of the firm, one other area of upper management responsibility is mentioned, namely, setting standards for vendors. The reason for placing this responsibility here is that IT staff may simply not have the business knowledge to recognize what to look for in a technical vendor. Standards involving the soundness of vendors, financial and otherwise, need to be set. It does no good to adopt a brilliant technical solution if the company able to maintain it disappears a few years after you start using it. The ethical principle involved here seems to be once again determining what the appropriate responsibilities are, given one's position. If you are an IT professional and those in other positions would not be able to fulfill an IT-related responsibility, then it must become yours.

For all the areas mentioned above, ethical issues can also arise in three circumstances: first, if the culture and/or policies are not being followed by the company; second, if the company culture and explicit policies are themselves unethical; and third, if the company culture and explicit policies conflict. We will return to these issues shortly in the section entitled "Partial Compliance."

Beyond the Organization

Because IT for an organization very often these days goes beyond the organization itself in supply chain management and outsourcing, multiple organizations may have to be considered and appropriate principles for settling potential conflicts need to be formulated. The principles involved will be discussed in Chapter VI, More Ethical Issues in a Market Economy. A typical arrangement might include suppliers being given inventory information from within the company and then being expected to manage internal inventory on the basis of pre-negotiated price levels. Wal-Mart, WestPoint Stevens, and Springs Industries are among companies using such Vendor-Managed-Inventory (VMI) arrangements extensively. Obviously, such an arrangement requires a great deal more trust than does the usual competitive bidding between suppliers. Each side must believe the other will fulfill its side of the bargain so that the other can get its benefits. The firm gets much more efficient inventory management with consequent potential lower prices, and the supplier gets a guaranteed, more predictable inventory stream that can also be managed more efficiently.

Insofar as VMI arrangements depend on the mutual recognition of both parties that they gain from observance of a cooperative agreement, they are, in effect, ethical agreements. However, insofar as one party complies more because of threats of harm, the agreement may no longer be ethical or even mutually beneficial. Wal-Mart, for example, in its zeal to produce the lowest prices possible and because of its dominant market share, can employ coercion against suppliers. The ethical considerations here involve monopoly and competition and will be dealt with in Chapter VI, More Ethical Issues in a Market Economy. Obviously, it is unethical to begin with a mutually beneficial agreement and then switch to a coercive one just because one is in a position to do so.

In addition, an organization (corporation or business) is embedded in a larger context. Therefore, it also has dealings with the society in which it does business, in which case the organization will need to deal with both internal personnel and outsiders as citizens with roles, rights and responsibilities that may conflict with the interests of the organization. Finally, over and above our role as participants in a particular human society is our role as human beings in the ongoing history of our species, and this role may engender conflicts with the dictates of one's society or the requirements of one's job. These issues will be considered in Section IV, Ultimate Questions, as well as in the next section.

Partial Compliance

Much of my discussion will proceed on the assumption that we are trying to discover the correct ethical principles for the situation and that these principles will be followed once they are acknowledged. In reality, correct ethical principles can fail to be followed for three kinds of reasons:

- **Ignorance or mistake:** the person acting either does not know the principle, gets the principle wrong, or gets the background facts wrong.
- **Shortcoming[1]:** the person acknowledges the correct principle but follows instead his own interests or some other lower level principle because he does not have the motivation to follow the correct principle for the case at hand
- **Evil:** the person is quite aware of the correct principle but believes he does not have to do the right thing.

In these cases of what we will call *partial compliance*, we can take two points of view: first, when we are the ones who are not complying; and second, when we have to manage or deal with others who are not complying. Although dealing well with any of these cases of partial compliance is likely to depend on details of the situation, there are some general remarks that may be helpful. In the case of one's self not complying, my remarks will be moral advice. In the case of others not complying, my remarks will be more in the nature of management suggestions.

If you are the one who is ignorant or mistaken about some ethical matter and thus have made a mistake or have faulty information, you need to consider the costs and benefits of being better informed on the matter or taking more care in reaching a decision. The fact that you have gotten this far in this book indicates you probably have a strong motivation to be better informed or to take more care about ethical matters. The mistakes or ignorance can be about the background information in the situation or about relevant ethical principles. In either case, the fault would be a failure of due diligence as appropriate to the situation. What you need to do is to figure out the appropriate level of diligence for the situation. No one has time to be completely informed about all situations, so it is necessary to decide how important the situation is. For mission-critical decisions, considerably more due diligence is called for. For example, some NASA managers on the occasion of the two shuttle failures apparently gave more weight to keeping on schedule than to potential threats to the lives of astronauts.

Similar considerations will apply if you are managing or otherwise responsible for someone who is ignorant or mistaken about some ethical matter. Extra investigation may be needed to determine an individual's opportunities to be informed. Although ignorance of the law may never be an excuse, ignorance of some relevant facts or principles may not be the individual's fault. "I had no idea I wasn't supposed to sell our address list to a competitor" will probably not fly, but "I had no idea that our outsourcing company falsified its credentials" may be acceptable as an excuse. Unfortunately, whether a mistake or ignorance is excusable does not always depend on the degree of due diligence. If the consequences are severe enough, due diligence may not be an excuse, and, conversely, if the organization is powerful enough, even behavior with very bad consequences may go unsanctioned.

If you are the one who falls short, you know what the ethical thing to do is but allow less-than-ethical self-interested motives to determine what you do. No one is perfect, and we all occasionally do things we are not proud of. If what is at stake is only your own inability to follow through on your own ethical convictions, the only advice would be to try to do better and to follow some sort of program of self-improvement. If falling short in doing ethical actions is frequent and characteristic for you, you are probably not reading this book.

The really difficult cases in this area are ones involving an unethical background environment, usually a company culture either encouraging or requiring unethical behavior. Your choice may be to comply with unethical orders or to quit. There may be an opportunity to be a whistle-blower, but, in spite of legal protections, this course of action usually costs the whistle-blower a fair amount. You may be lucky enough to be able to cause the unethical behavior to change within the company without damaging your own prospects in the company. But one can't count on this happening.

It is easy to say that the right thing to do is to refuse to obey unethical orders. It is easy to say because it is true. Yet for those workers whose fates depend on the judgment of possibly unethical higher-ups, the disruption to one's career and to family that may be caused by this refusal require careful consideration. It may be that refusal is more than one can be ethically required to do. But then again, in some circumstances, it may be ethically required. It may be what is called *supererogatory*, meaning literally "above what is asked." I will call such actions *heroic* because "supererogatory" is a real mouthful. This is a stretch of meaning because heroic actions normally involve ignoring a serious threat to one's own well-being. *Heroic* in our sense will mean simply that the action is more than what is ethically required.

What, then, are your ethical obligations in an environment when others are not complying? It will often be used as a justification that in a competitive environment, one company cannot afford to behave ethically or even seriously consider behaving ethically when such behavior would produce a serious competitive disadvantage. This justification is mentioned frequently in discussions of offshoring. If all my competitors are reducing their costs by sending many of their IT services to India or China, I will be at a competitive disadvantage if I don't do so. In fact, I may even be failing to do my duty to my company and its stockholders or stakeholders.

The relevant ethical consideration here is that, whatever you ultimately do, the higher level principle has to be acknowledged by what you do (Schultz, 1971).[2] In the case of offshoring, the fact that it would be a severe competitive disadvantage not to offshore is ethically relevant, but it is not decisive. This particular issue will be discussed at length in Chapter VII, Offshoring as an Ethical Issue. The critical point is that, even if reasons of interest make it difficult or impossible for you or your company to do what you believe is ethical, it is still necessary to acknowledge your own ethical principle in what you do.

It is easy to see why. If the fact that other people are not behaving well was a sufficient reason for you not to behave well, the situation could never improve. But fortunately people are ethically optimistic and in most circumstances believe that improvement is possible. Of course, it may be foolhardy and completely unproductive to do the right thing in circumstances where ethical principles do not hold sway. It may also be heroic, but heroism is not ethically required. The word mentioned before was "supererogatory," more than what can be asked of a person.

The chances are very slim that you are an *evil* person reading this book, because long before now you would have decided that ethics is simply not something with which you need concern yourself. The only reason you might be reading this book is to get the jump on those who, for some reason or other, consider ethical considerations to be important. Actually, there is probably very little that can be said to such persons because they are very likely to suffer from the character disorder of *sociopathy*. In general, sociopaths can't really appreciate the reality of other human beings with the same needs as theirs. Therefore, they are permanently at Kohlberg's Stage Two (Kohlberg, 1976).[3] Unfortunately, sociopathy is difficult or impossible to treat or to cure, and sociopaths frequently spend large parts of their lives in prisons. Some, however, are very successful. Very often they are quite charming and do well as salesman or actors (Cleckley, 1988).[4]

So the more likely relevant advice would be about how to deal with sociopaths in your environment. And the best advice would be: Don't cross paths with a sociopath. What makes sociopaths so extraordinarily difficult to deal with is that they can be extremely intelligent and, in fact, give the appearance of complying with ethical standards when they think that would best further their interests. Then, from your point of view, they suddenly betray you, but from their point of view, it is business as usual. The management of a corporation like Enron could well have been largely sociopathic.

Conclusion

This concludes the background needed for discussion of ethical problems raised by IT. Many of these issues depend upon considerations of justice within society and among societies. Some of them depend upon more general ethical considerations. Some principles will need to be developed as the discussion unfolds, but they will always have a basis in the general features of ethical theory outlined in this section and in Rawls' Principles of Justice (Rawls, 1999).

References

Applegate, L. M., Austin, R. D., & McFarlan, F. W. (2003). *Corporate information systems: Text and cases*. 6th ed. New York: McGraw-Hill Irwin.

Cleckley, H. (1988). *The mask of sanity*. Augusta, GA: Emily S. Cleckley.

Kohlberg, L. (1976). Moral stages and moralization. In T. Lickona (Ed.), *Moral development and behavior* (pp. 31-53). New York: Holt, Rinehart & Winston.

Rawls, J. (1999). *A theory of justice* (rev.ed.). Cambridge, MA: Harvard University Press.

Endnotes

[1]   In most ethical writings in English, the term used is "weakness." The original Greek concept is *akrasia,* which literally means lack of power.

[2]   See Chapter II, A Background in Ethical Theory, "The Rational Basis of Ethics."

[3]   See Chapter I, Ethical Issues in Information Technology, "Determining Right and Wrong."

[4]   The remark about sociopaths as successful salesman and actors is from personal communication with the Los Angeles psychiatrist, Dr. William Goldsmith.

Section II

Ethics and
IT Professionals

Chapter IV

Professional Duties

It is perhaps easiest to begin the application of ethics to information technology with the ethical responsibilities of IT professionals. Several ethical codes have been developed, and in this chapter we will see how the concepts of Part I apply to these codes. My aim is to establish the ethical basis of these codes. The underlying ethical concepts are Rawlsian, but not his Principles of Justice (Rawls, 1999). Rather, they are distinctions developed as part of the theory of right action. The distinction between duty and obligation is particularly relevant. In addition, something needs to be said about the concept of a *profession*.

Most IT professionals have a very strong sense of their responsibilities as IT professionals. In a way, it is astonishing that such a young profession has developed such a strong sense of its own ethical identity so quickly. Older professions such as Medicine or Law have traditions going back over two thousand years, and their standards have been incorporated into law in most areas. Although IT has its professional organizations, such as the Association for Computing Machinery (ACM) and the Association of Information Technology Professionals (AITP), those organizations do not currently perform a widely recognized credentialing function. Although these organizations promulgate model curricula, they have nothing like the force of the American Medical Association (AMA) certification for medical schools, or the American Bar Association (ABA) certification of law schools.

Since IT is a profession without benefit of the formal apparatus of the older professions, it follows that the credentialing and legal sanctions of the older professions are not what makes them professions. Credentialing and legal sanctions safeguard what was already there, namely a *calling* shared by individuals. Professions differ from mere jobs because those in professions commit themselves indefinitely toward serving a goal beyond their own self-interest, which is their primary focus. Thus, those in the medical profession commit themselves to healing people, and those in the law commit themselves to interpreting and applying the law and preserving the integrity of the legal process. Professional athletes similarly commit themselves to practicing their sport as well as they can. All professionals are prepared to set aside their individual interests when their profession requires it. The basis of a profession—an individually adopted goal beyond self-interest—is also the essential basis for professional ethics.[1]

What then is this goal for IT professionals? What do IT professionals feel *called* to do? I think their calling is to provide the best functioning IT systems (infrastructure and applications) possible in the organizational context in which they are dealing. In terms of this calling, IT professionals know what they need to take responsibility for in the technical area, even when managers or clients have other ideas. These responsibilities are often not mandated by management. Indeed, management may not even be aware that IT professionals have assumed and carried out these responsibilities. Yet the well-being of the organization may very well depend on these responsibilities being carried out. A good example is data integrity; nonprofessionals usually have only a vague idea of what is involved in insuring data integrity, and yet failures in insuring data integrity will almost certainly compromise the usability of a system.

Even without formal, generally accepted credentialing for IT professionals, there is still a distinct calling recognized by IT professionals with duties attached to it. The absence of generally accepted credentialing does, however, create possibilities for conflicts with management and others, which we will discuss later in this chapter.

IT Professional Ethics

Ethics in the most comprehensive sense includes character, the rightness and wrongness of actions, the value or goodness of things and situations, and the justness of institutions. In professional ethics, we are concerned with character and right or wrong actions. For professional ethics, two important types of right action are fulfilling obligations and carrying out duties. Obligations stem from agreements and are distinguished from duties, which we acquire when we assume a given role whether we have an agreement or not. The distinction is not merely terminological. For an obligation to exist, you must have agreed to do something. To have a duty, no agreement is necessary—it comes with the territory of being a mother, a citizen, an employee, or an IT professional.

Ethics looks for principles that would resolve conflicting interests. Most people would agree on some version of doing the greatest good for the greatest number or some version of the Golden Rule; that is, to act on principles to which everyone could agree. In most cases, the answers will be similar using either approach.[2]

I analyzed three codes of professional ethics in terms of these ethical distinctions: the Association of Computer Machinery (ACM) Code of Ethics (1992), the Association of Information Technology Professionals (AITP) Code of Ethics (2002), and the Software Engineer's Code of Ethics and Professional Practice (SEC) developed jointly by the ACM and the Computer Society of the Institute of Electrical and Electronic Engineers (IEEE CS) (1998). First, I will state and discuss the composite ethical conclusion and then briefly discuss the special features of each code. IT professionals have:

1. ethical duties as citizens and as ethical persons;
2. duties and obligations as employees (or contractors) to their employers;
3. enabling professional duties, things they have to do in order to maintain their status as professionals (These duties are to the profession and to other IT professionals);
4. substantive duties to their users; and
5. substantive system duties (infrastructure and application).

Each category has a different ethical basis and status. Most are duties, but are based on different roles. The distinction between enabling and substantive duties is important: *Enabling* duties are things one has to do in order to maintain one's status in a profession, for example, in IT, by staying current. *Substantive* duties are things one actually has to do in the line of practice of one's profession.

The first two categories—duties as citizens or ethical persons and ethical requirements as employees—are not specific to IT professionals and need to be mentioned only when the IT context requires special attention. Ethical considerations of conflicts of interest and using employer's resources for one's own purposes perhaps come up more often in IT contexts. Broader social or ethical implications of IT development also need to be considered. Most duties and obligations as employees are also not specifically IT professional duties, although their performance is important to maintaining the integrity of the profession. Confidentiality and not misusing resources are perhaps general duties of special importance in an IT context.

Enabling professional duties need to be performed either to keep one's own place in the profession, working toward the goal of the calling, or enabling or enhancing the profession itself. Knowledge-related duties are especially important for IT. Keeping up with the rapid changes in IT is a daunting proposition. It is not uncommon for IT professionals to spend significant portions of their free time "keeping current." "Keeping current" is essential for being able to fulfill the goals of the profession, as well as do one's job well. Also, the IT codes of ethics all address the importance of making the existence of the profession and its special expertise and goals known to the public as well as to managers and employers. They also address promoting quality work within IT and cooperation between fellow professionals toward reaching professional goals. In this area, there are potentially difficult and destructive conflicts between proprietary information and the needs of the profession. An important function of patent and copyright is to provide legitimate protection for the originator of the idea to make it possible to recoup development costs and exploit legitimate competitive advantage. But keeping certain information proprietary can stifle growth as well. These issues will be discussed further in Chapter V, Justice in a Market Economy, and Chapter IX, Copyright and Piracy.

Finally, there are substantive IT professional duties. To the users: IT professionals have the duty to include all affected by a system in requirements design and implementation. Also, they have a duty not to misuse their technical expertise in dealing with those less knowledgeable. To management: IT professionals have the duty to provide whatever information and expertise they can toward keeping projects on time and on budget.[3] I would count this as a substantive professional IT duty just because the track record of IT projects being on time and on budget is so poor.[4] If an IT professional needs to be reminded of anything, it is this: Substantive system duties include helping to maintain data integrity, being responsible for appropriate maintenance standards, and, more generally, ensuring appropriate ongoing support for systems implemented.[5] These are duties that an IT professional needs to aware of even when management may not have much understanding of their importance. Management failure to support data integrity and appropriate support may require protest if management chooses to ignore them to the possible detriment of the entire system.

Some other substantive items in the codes may not be duties but, rather, valuable things to achieve that are not ethical requirements. Examples may include designing and implementing systems that enhance the quality of the work environment, and defining good and bad uses of the system—both from the ACM code. It would be *better* if IT professionals accomplished these things, but they are not *unethical* if they fail to do these things.

This raises the question whether any of these substantive professional considerations are ethical requirements at all. How can keeping projects on time and on budget be an ethical duty? I believe it is—for an IT professional. As I observed at the beginning of the chapter, the lack of accepted credentialing authorities is not essential for the existence of a profession. What is essential is a shared *calling*, a shared goal transcending individual self-interest. I believe IT professionals have and share such a goal, namely, to provide the best functioning IT systems possible in the organizational context in which they are dealing. If you accept this goal, as an employee or consultant, then the duties and obligations just discussed become ethical requirements for you.

Three Codes of Ethics

Following are some of the details of the three codes of IT professional ethics that yielded the results just discussed. The codes I will examine are the ACM Code of Ethics, the AITP Code of Ethics, and the Software Engineer's Code of Ethics.

ACM Code of Ethics

The ACM Code in its current form dates from 1992, with revisions up to 2004. The ACM Code is divided into four sections, General Ethical Considerations, Specific IT Professional Responsibilities, Leadership Responsibilities, and principles for complying with the code. (The code is available at www.acm.org/constitution/code.html.) The second and third sections list professional IT duties and managerial duties. These include both enabling and substantive duties. The last section discusses compliance conditions for the code. This code is very good in what it mentions but is somewhat incomplete.

The Code's "General Moral Imperatives" are (using the numbering in the Code):

1.1   Contribute to society and human well-being;

1.2   Avoid harm to others (includes substantive duty of assessing social consequences of systems);

1.3   Be honest and trustworthy;

1.4   Be fair and take action not to discriminate;

1.5   Honor property rights including copyright and patent;

1.6   Give proper credit for intellectual property;

1.7   Respect the privacy of others (includes substantive responsibility for data integrity); and

1.8   Honor confidentiality.

The first four items are compatible with both utilitarian and duty-based ethical theories, and include considerations of justice in the imperative to be fair and take action not to discriminate.[6] Item 1.2 also includes an interesting discussion about the professional responsibility of assessing the social consequences of systems and possible whistle-blowing if management does not act to mitigate dangerous consequences. In discussion of Items 1.5 and 1.6, the code extends property rights to require authorization for any duplication and extends proper credit to include cases where there has not been explicit protection by copyright or other legal means. The discussion of privacy in Item 1.7 includes a responsibility for the integrity of data, which I previously instanced as a clear professional IT responsibility, as well as guidelines for the handling of data to protect privacy. The discussion of confidentiality in Item 1.8 mentions keeping explicit agreements but also extends it to any information not directly related to performance of one's duties.

The next sections, listing professional IT duties and managerial duties, are mainly important duties enabling one to function as an IT professional. Important substantive duties are spelled out in the discussion sections. I classify these duties as: *enabling* duties that enable one to fulfill one's calling as an IT professional; *ethical* duties; and *substantive* duties, which spell out ethical requirements specifically for IT professionals.

2.1 Strive for quality (enabling)

2.2 Maintain professional competence (enabling)

2.4 Provide for professional review (enabling)

2.3 Obey laws relevant to professional work (ethical)

2.6 Honor agreements (ethical) (includes a substantive duty of personal accountability for work)

2.7 Improve public understanding (enabling)

2.8 Use IT resources only when authorized (employee?)

3.1 Act appropriately with respect to social impacts of IT (enabling)

3.2 Design and build systems that enhance the quality of work environment (substantive)

3.3 Define good and bad uses of the system and help enforce policies to support this. (substantive)

3.4 Include all affected by a system in requirements design and implementation. (substantive)

3.5 Systems should not demean users (?)

3.6 Provide learning opportunities for other professionals. (enabling)

Two items are puzzling to me: Although Item 2.8, the directive to use IT resources only when authorized, seems correct, I am not sure of its basis. It seems to be a duty of every employee to use organizational resources only when authorized for work purposes. Surfing the Net on company time, however common, is still not ethical. Yet a database consultant would probably have a broader scope of authorization than a data entry clerk—as well as more potential to get to more of the system. So although the basis of the requirement is one's role as an employee, the fact that the requirement comes with extra permissions and limitations for an IT professional may be a reason for including this directive as an IT-specific duty.

Also, I have a hard time thinking of examples for Item 3.5, the requirement that systems should not demean users. Systems can be developed that include overly technical or complex language for the users, but this is simply bad, inappropriate design. For such a system to be demeaning, it would have to be done with intentional contempt for the less- educated user. Although this may happen, it has not appeared in my experience.

Because these professional duties were generated as a list without priorities, it is hard to be confident about how complete they are. As with other lists of ethical requirements, such as the Ten Commandments, we need a way to resolve conflicts.[7] And to resolve conflicts, we probably need to adopt an ethical theory. Without a background theory, we don't have a general way to resolve very possible real conflicts—for example, between contributing to well-being and avoiding harm, or between being fair and avoiding harm. The authors of the code show awareness of this problem. For example, the commentary on Item 1.4, the ethical duty to be fair and take action not to discriminate, makes clear that correcting a violation of equal opportunity in the use of computer resources "does not provide a basis for the violation of any other ethical imperatives of the code" (ACM, 1992). So fairness comes out as the least important of the ethical considerations. This conclusion is probably correct in most cases, because violations of fairness and equal opportunity can often only be meaningfully addressed at the institutional level of laws and court decisions. But suppose we have a case of racial discrimination in a promotion or job assignment, and evidence for discriminatory treatment is contained in documents protected by a confidentiality agreement. The correct ethical decision in this case is not clear cut, as the code would have it.

AITP Code of Ethics

The Association of Information Technology Professionals (AITP) Code of Ethics is addressed to IT professionals generally. It is framed in terms of "obligations to" four stakeholders: management, fellow IT professionals, society, and employers. Users of IT are not explicitly mentioned as a potential ethically relevant group, but the Code does mention an important ethical consideration involving users. (The AITP Code can be found at www.aitp.org.)

The AITP Code uses the term "obligation" in a nonstandard way. Ordinarily, obligations stem from agreements and are distinguished from duties, which we acquire when we assume a given role whether we have an agreement or not. (These distinctions are discussed in Chapter II, A Background in Ethical Theory, in the section, "Rights, Duties, Obligations.") The distinction is not merely terminological—it makes a difference for the basis of an obligation or duty. For example, the AITP Code mentions respect for confidentiality in a section on obligation to society. But the scope of confidentiality varies significantly between organizations—some treat almost all information as competitive and hence not to be disseminated, whereas others require open exchange of information to function. So what is properly an obligation to confidentiality is based on keeping a confidentiality agreement specific to the organization.[8] In this case, the AITP Code does correctly identify the item of concern as an obligation, but attributes the obligation to the wrong stakeholder—the obligation is really to the organization, not society, and its content is determined by the organization's confidentiality agreement.

On the other hand, the AITP Code mentions not taking advantage of the lack of knowledge or inexperience on the part of others under an "obligation to management." This seems rather to be a special duty of an IT professional, to be observed regardless of employment or consulting agreements with an employer or management. One acquires the duty when one adopts the calling of IT professional. The duty also seems to extend to users as well as management.

The following table (Table 1) is my reorganization of the ethical considerations of the AITP Code. They are sorted by ethical type (character trait, duty, or obligation). Also, like items have been combined, and the last column replaces "obligation to" in the original AITP Code. I believe "who benefits" is closer to what the AITP had in mind.

Reorganized in this way, most of the ethical considerations listed in the AITP Code turn out to be what I am calling "duties." Again, the terminology, in and of itself, is not important. The difference between a duty and an obligation is that an obligation is something one assumes by an agreement, often explicit; whereas a duty is something one is subject to as soon as one assumes a role.[9] (A "calling' is also a role). The last three items on the reorganized list are obligations: The obligation to obey the laws is based on what is often called tacit consent, namely, continuing to live in the country and accept its benefits (Locke, 1690). The obligation to uphold the bylaws of AITP and to cooperate is based on an individual's agreement to be a member. And the obligation to uphold confidentiality is based on an employee's agreement with his or her employer.

All the other preceding considerations are different. The first two call for the character trait of honesty and its exercise in not falsely claiming credit for others' work. This is worth reminding people of and serves to separate the IT profession from the dishonest professions of thievery, drug dealing, and so on.[10] But it may not be necessary to include this specifically in a professional code

Table 1. Ethical considerations of the AITP Code of Ethics

	Stakeholder	Action or behavior	Basis	Who benefits
Character trait	Bearer	Honesty and fairness	Ethical person	Everyone
Duty to	Bearer	Not take credit for others work	Ethical person	Fellow AITP members & Profession
Duty to	Employer	• Avoid conflict of interest • Protect proper employer interests • Not misrepresent or withhold relevant knowledge • Not to use employer resources for own purposes	Role: Employee	Employer
Duty to	Organization	Accept responsibility and not misuse authority	Role: Employee or manager	Organization
Duty to	Profession	• Promote management understanding of IT. • Disseminate IT knowledge. Keep IT knowledge up to date. • Not misrepresent IT capabilities • Cooperate in identifying and solving IT problems • Not to exploit systems weaknesses for own purposes	Calling: IT professional	Profession, Management, Employer, Society
Duty to	Profession	Act against illegal or unethical IT	Calling: IT professional	Fellow AITP members & Profession
Duty to	Users	Not take advantage of lack of knowledge	Calling: IT professional	Profession, Management, Users
Obligation to	Country	Obey laws	Citizen	Society
Obligation to	Members	Uphold bylaws & cooperate with members	Membership in AITP	Fellow AITP members
Obligation to	Organization, Employer	Uphold confidentiality	Confidentiality agreement for organization	Employer

of ethics. Perhaps the general statement that ethical behavior is, of course, expected of IT professionals would be sufficient.

The remaining duties are owed to three basic groups: Employers, the IT Profession, and Users. The duties to employers one acquires by becoming an employee. The duty to accept responsibility and not misuse authority requires a bit more, namely, that one be given authority as employee or manager. But all of these duties to employers are duties of *every* employee—namely avoiding conflicts of interest, protecting employer interests, not misrepresenting or withholding knowledge, and not using employer resources for one's own purposes. They are indeed duties because one can't get out of them by saying that one didn't agree to them or no one told me about them. Someone who says "No one told me not to make phone calls to my aunt in the Ukraine on the company dime," is not likely to be an employee for long. Again, because these are definitely not specific to IT professionals, it is not obvious that they belong in a code of IT professional ethics.

However, it may once again be that these areas need to be brought to the attention of IT professionals because IT professionals have more opportunity to transgress in these areas. Conflicts of interest and using employer resources for one's own purposes can arise in unexpected ways within an IT professional context, and so special care may need to be taken to avoid them. So it may be worth including them in a code of IT professional ethics.

The remaining duties are definitely good candidates for ethical responsibilities, specifically of the IT professional:

- To promote management understanding of IT;
- To disseminate IT knowledge;
- Not to misrepresent IT capabilities;
- To cooperate in identifying and solving IT problems; and
- Not to exploit system weaknesses for one's own purposes.

All except the last are what I called *enabling* duties—they enable the IT professional to fulfill his or her calling. The last is a substantive duty of IT professionals. Not all professions would endorse a requirement not to exploit system weaknesses—part of what lawyers do is to exploit weaknesses in the legal system.

So, in fact, the AITP Code really includes only one substantive IT professional duty, as well as some enabling duties for IT professionals and many general duties.

Software Engineering Code of Ethics and Professional Practice

The Software Engineering Code of Ethics and Professional Practice (SEC) (1998), developed by a joint task force of the Computer Society of the Institute of Electrical and Electronic Engineers (IEEE-CS) and the ACM, focuses on

Software Engineering as the relevant profession. Because this code is very much aware of software engineering as embedded in an IT context, it is helpful in identifying more general IT professional duties. The SEC consists of eight principles that express ethically responsible relationships related to software development. Each of those principles gives rise to obligations (or, I would add, duties) that are "founded in the software engineer's humanity, special care owed to people affected by the work of software engineers, and the unique elements of the practice of Software Engineering" (SEEP Executive Committee, 1998).

The eight principles are that software engineers shall:

1. **Public:** Act consistently with the public interest.

2. **Client and employer:** Act in the best interests of their client and employer consistent with 1.

3. **Product:** Ensure products meet highest professional standards.

4. **Judgment:** Maintain integrity and independence of professional judgment.

5. **Management:** (SE managers and leaders shall:) manage software development and maintenance ethically.

6. **Profession:** Advance integrity and reputation of profession consistent with 1.

7. **COLLEAGUES.** Support colleagues.

8. **SELF.** Participate in lifelong learning and promote an ethical approach to profession.

This SEC actually contains very little specific to software development. Most of the requirements are formulated at the level of an IT development project, which would apply across the board to most all IT professionals. This Code also includes a number of prioritizations to help settle conflicts. For example, Number 2, the best interests of client and employer, as well as Number 6, the best interests of the profession, are explicitly superseded by Number 1, the public interest.

The code's Public, Client and Employer, and Judgment sections parallel similar sections on general ethical concerns in the other two codes: Software engineers should recognize that their work has to serve the public good, avoid being dangerous and causing harm. Issues of fair access to software should be addressed. A concern not addressed in the other codes is professional skills should be volunteered to good causes. Two items also not found in the other codes: specifically not to use software obtained or retained illegally; and no interest detrimental to employer or client is to be promoted, including outside work, except when a higher ethical principle is at stake.

The section on PRODUCT includes specifics not found in the other codes that definitely belong in a list of professional IT duties:

- Take responsibility for understanding and documenting specifications and insuring that specs meet user requirements and have appropriate approvals;
- Ensure realistic estimates of project costs, scheduling, personnel, quality, and outcomes together with probability of success or failure;
- Use only ethically obtained data;
- Help maintain data integrity; and
- Be responsible for appropriate maintenance.

As you can see, all of these apply to IT development generally, not just to software.

The Management section is unusual. It states the ethical responsibilities of *managers* of IT, including due process for disputes and fairness in employment. Besides fair compensation, hiring, and ownership agreements, managers are to respect the IT professional's ethical concern and the Code itself. The directive to ensure realistic project estimates is included here too. These directives are obligations and duties owed *to* IT professionals, rather than obligations and duties *of* IT professionals. These responsibilities will be discussed shortly in the section on "Management Conflicts."

The final sections on Profession, Colleagues, and Self are mainly devoted to *enabling* duties that enable an individual to function well as a professional: mutual support, honesty, and keeping current. A striking concern not present in the other codes is that the SEC is to be taken as definitive of ethical behavior for a software engineer, and the Code itself is to be promoted as an ethical standard within and without the profession. Although this is a laudable goal, considerably more institutional backup is probably necessary to make it stick, probably including widely accepted credentialing for IT professionals. However, recent attempts to license IT professionals have met with ACM opposition[11] (Reynolds 2003).

Management Conflicts

Although the professional Software Engineering Code (SEC) has the right idea, it is probably too much to expect management to adhere to a professional code not widely accepted as a standard within the profession itself. So the pertinent issue is how to deal with management when there is a conflict between management's demands and ethical IT professional behavior. One major difference between IT professionals and doctors, lawyers, or other professionals is that nonprofessionals in the medical or legal area usually defer to doctors or lawyers in the areas of their expertise. It is up to a doctor to determine what is medically possible in the circumstances, and lawyers have the authority to inform clients about what is legally possible. But for IT professionals, this area of authority or expertise is not generally acknowledged.

The development of the automated baggage handling system at the Denver International Airport is a classic case of conflict between management and IT professionals (Applegate, Montealegre, Nelson, & Knoop, 1996). The developer of the baggage system, BAE Systems, accepted the development contract with several stipulated conditions. Possibly most important of these were a cutoff date for revisions to the system and priority access to physical locations necessary for the system. Management simply ignored these requirements, presumably out of ignorance of the likelihood of schedule slippage. A system test for PR purposes was actually scheduled without notifying the developers in advance! Needless to say, the results were disastrous. Baggage was actually mangled by the system. The final result—the opening of the airport was delayed for over a year. The airport sued BAE, but eventually BAE took over maintenance of the replacement (non-automated) baggage system.

This case and other cases of conflict between IT professionals and management bring home the lesson that it takes more than a code of ethics to insure good working relations between the two. It also takes more than upfront specification of appropriate conditions for system management. In the Denver case, it was probably a mistake for the IT firm to accept the contract. But it is hard to tell how much is hindsight in this observation—there were management changes detrimental to a successful project part way through the development period.

It may also be a substantive duty of an IT professional to determine whether management will be able to provide the support to IT developers to achieve their project goals in a manner consistent with the goals and ethics of their profession. If the answer is that management cannot provide such support, we may find ourselves in the area of partial compliance discussed in Chapter III, namely, how to behave ethically when others are not.

References

Applegate, L., Montealegre, R., Nelson, H. J., & Knoop, C.-I. 1996. BAE automated systems: Denver International Airport baggage-handling system. *Harvard Business School Case 396-311*. Cambridge, MA: Harvard Business School Press.

Association for Computing Machinery (ACM). (1992). ACM code of ethics and professional conduct. Retrieved on August 22, 2004, from http://www.acm.org/constitution/code.html

Association of Information Technology Professionals (AITP). (2002). AITP Code of Ethics. Retrieved on August 22, 2004, from http://www.aitp.org

Gibbs, W. W. (1994). Software's chronic crisis. *Scientific American,* September, 86-100.

Locke, J. (1690). *The second treatise of government.* Retrieved on August 22, 2004, from http://www.constitution.org/jl/2ndtreat.htm

Rawls, J. (1999). *A theory of justice* (rev. ed.). Cambridge, MA: Harvard University Press.

Reynolds, G. (2003). *Ethics in information technology.* Boston, MA: Course Technology.

SEEP Executive Committee. (1999). Software engineer's code of ethics and professional practice. *Institute of Electrical and Electronic Engineers (IEEE).* Retrieved on August 22, 2004, from http://www.ieee.org

Endnotes

1   My thanks to Major Johnson for calling my attention to the importance of considering the *nature* of a profession.

2   See Chapter II, A Background in Ethical Theory, "Rights, Duties, Obligations" and "Theories of Right" for a fuller discussion.

3   The SEC Code makes this also a duty of management itself, but it is unclear what force an IT professional requirement can have for a manager not in the profession.

4   Numerous commentators have made this observation throughout the years, for example, Gibbs (1994).

5   My thanks to David Mill for pointing out that ensuring appropriate system support should be a duty.

6   See Chapter II, A Background in Ethical Theory, beginning sections.

7   Ibid.

8   In the absence of an agreement, there is still an obligation not to cause the company harm by disseminating information that would clearly cause harm, for example, giving customer lists to competitors. The basis for this obligation is an employee's agreement to work for the company.

9   See Chapter II, A Background in Ethical Theory, section on "Rights, Duties, Obligations."

10   Although we speak of professional thieves, thieves often lack any goal beyond self-interest. So it is not clear that these occupations deserve the name of profession in the first place.

11   Opposition to licensing is based on the fact that there is neither an accepted canonical body of knowledge nor an administrative body to provide oversight. To some extent, there may be a chicken-and-egg problem here.

Chapter V

Justice in a Market Economy

As we saw from the last two chapters, the ethical IT professional is embedded in contexts of management, organization, and society. Ethical behavior for the IT professional is, therefore, impacted by the ethics of people and institutions in his or her environment. The primary term for ethical institutions is *justice*.[1] In the next three chapters, we will examine the justice of institutions impacting the IT professional. The framework used will be that provided by the works of John Rawls (1999, 2001).

Rawls' work is based on the idea of a social contract, that a justly ordered society is one to which individuals can freely decide to obligate themselves. But our decision will very likely be biased if we base it on our current situation. So Rawls' major addition is to say that the decision must be made prior to being in society, without knowledge of what our position will be in society, and it will be a decision we will be obligated to stick to and expect others to make and stick to as well. The basic principles for society chosen in this position (which Rawls calls the *original position*) will be the Principles of Justice. According to Rawls (1999, 2001), there will be two:

1. **The First Principle of Justice or Greatest Equal Liberty:** Society is to be arranged so that all members have the greatest equal liberty possible for all, including fair equality of opportunity. Each individual has basic liberties which are not to be compromised or traded off for other benefits.

Besides the basic freedoms such as freedom of speech, assembly, religion, and so on, it includes equality of opportunity. Thus society's rules are not biased against anyone in it and allow all to pursue their interests and realize their abilities.

2.   **The Second Principle of Justice or the Difference Principle:** Economic inequalities in society are justified insofar as they make members of the least advantaged social class, better off than if there were no inequality. The social contract basis for this principle is straightforward: If you are entering a society with no knowledge of your specific place in that society, the Difference Principle guarantees that you will be no worse off than you need to be to keep the society functioning.

Market Economies

From the point of view of Rawls' Principles of Justice (1999, 2001), a market economy has very positive features. Competition in a market economy produces very efficient economic results, and it does so without administrative overhead—through the well-known "invisible hand"—with communication of prices and market share taking place through the market itself. Thus, when Dell entered the PC market in the late 1980s, other major suppliers were charging about $1500 for a basic PC. Dell was able to charge about half that price and still make a profit. The other major suppliers lost market share and were forced to lower their prices to regain market share and stay competitive.

It was, of course, important that the PCs being sold by the different vendors had the same features and were of similar quality. In addition to Dell, there have been lower priced PCs with either poorer quality or features and, perhaps most important, poorer technical support for problems. Lower priced PCs of lower quality with poor support would have a much smaller tendency to force overall prices lower. Dell did pay attention to these items, and the result was that competition in a market economy produced a better allocation of resources— the market showed that the older vendors were charging too much for their computers. Some of that excess was transferred to computer consumers in the form of savings.

So a market economy is a very good candidate to be a background institution in a just society. Its efficiency—in the sense of no one being able to be better off without someone else being worse off—goes a long way toward satisfying the Second Principle of Justice, the Difference Principle. Efficiency in a market economy means that there is no slack—increasing the share of one group will mean that another group will lose.[2] And no administrative overhead means that there are more resources to distribute.

Economists and social theorists accept that justice (or "equity") is more than efficiency.[3] Suppose Rupert Murdoch were to achieve the situation where he has all the economic goods and everyone else has nothing (he seems to be trying). This distribution would be efficient—he would lose if any economic goods were transferred to anyone else—but it would hardly be just. The requirements of the Difference Principle, in addition to efficiency, are discussed in Chapter II, A Background in Ethical Theory, in the section entitled "Theory of Justice." For the present discussion, two points need to be kept in mind: First, we regard a market economy as a means to satisfy the principles of justice, primarily the Difference Principle, rather than an institution ethically justified on its own. Violations of competitiveness solely for the sake of increased benefit overall are simply not justified from the point of view of justice. It is even worse when those already more advantaged are the only ones to benefit. Second, the basic idea of the Principles of Justice is to ensure fair conditions of social and economic cooperation to which all can agree. A market economy's efficiency must always be tempered by the Difference Principle's requirement that the least advantaged cannot be required to sacrifice any more than is necessary to keep the society running; otherwise, the least advantaged could not agree to a social contract and we would not have a just society.

A market economy is subject to distortions that destroy its efficiency (and its status as a just institution) unless there are external forces that can keep it efficient. One major distortion is monopoly. If a company becomes the sole supplier for a type of good, it can set much higher prices and pay much less attention to customer requirements than if a competitive environment is present. The same thing happens when a group of suppliers collude on higher prices, the situation called *oligopoly*. When competition does not set prices, there is no guarantee of efficiency. Also, the companies involved are almost certainly getting more than their fair share of income and wealth, thus violating the Difference Principle.

Honest behavior in a market economy is, oddly enough, in some ways contrary in spirit to ethical behavior. In a market economy, we are required to behave in a purely self-interested and rational way and explicitly required *not* to cooperate. Cooperative solutions such as collusion and price-fixing are considered dishonest behavior in a free market context. So not all cooperative agreements are ethical or just, even though virtually all ethical principles are based on cooperative agreements to limit one's self-interest.[4]

American society is not based upon a market economy as the primary ethical justification for social rules, even in economic matters. As we noted, a market economy is a good candidate to be part of the economic structure in a just society because of its efficiency and low overhead. But without some social constraints, an unregulated market economy can allow monopolies, which have no competitive pressure to be efficient, to respond to the needs of customers, or to price goods in a fair way. It is perhaps surprising that recent U.S. government administrations of both parties have been so lax in preventing monopolistic or oligopolistic mergers. Because of the central role of a competitive market economy in realizing justice, it looks as though they have abandoned justice for the sake of apparent efficiency—or worse, the greater well-being of those better off.

In this chapter, we will consider the most striking example of a monopolistic IT company, Microsoft; the efforts to correct dysfunctional monopoly; arguments that Microsoft's apparent monopoly is not dysfunctional at all; what the relevant just (ethical) social policies could be; and the ethical consequences for those of us who are neither monopolists nor makers of social policy. At the end of the chapter, we will discuss IT-related aspects of the Difference Principle not connected with a market economy.[5]

A Brief History of Microsoft

Almost all commentators agree that Microsoft is primarily a fast follower in the IT world rather than a first-mover innovator. At the beginning, Bill Gates did not write MS-DOS; rather, the program was acquired from someone else, spiffed up, and sold to IBM—with a proviso for a royalty to Microsoft on each copy of the software sold.

There is nothing wrong per se in being a fast follower. As historians of IT have pointed out, fast followers, those second in the innovative line, usually prosper much better than first-mover innovators because market forces are usually much clearer and consumers have been educated by the time the fast followers enter the marketplace. Fast followers do not have quite so many lumps to take.

In fact, IBM itself was a fast follower, and much more successful than its predecessor UNIVAC.

Of course, IT companies, especially large ones, want to have innovation as part of their image, especially for marketing purposes, even if they are, in fact, fast followers. Over the years, IBM, as a fast follower, generated reams of vaporware and paper initiatives that ultimately amounted to nothing. One striking example is AD/Cycle, a systems development initiative discussed extensively in the early 1990s.[6] IBM was primarily a solutions aggregator and hardware and software manufacturer, and, back in the mainframe era, was marketing reliability rather than innovation per se. Nevertheless, some of their solutions became de facto standards, such as CICS for transaction processing systems. My point is that there is often cognitive dissonance between the claims of innovativeness by fast followers and their actual achievements.

IBM also brings up the second point, namely, the role of competition and competitiveness in the behavior of fast followers. Microsoft evidently learned an important lesson from IBM in keeping the rights to the MS-DOS software. At about the same time, IBM had adopted what is called "open architecture" for PC hardware, with the result that a competing clone market rose rapidly and, in fact, IBM totally lost control of standards for the PC. At one point, IBM's own PCs were said to be "not fully IBM compatible." This was not at all bad for IT and certainly played a major role in driving down the cost of PCs—the usual benefit of intense competition. But it was not so good for IBM, who eventually went out of the (desktop) PC hardware business altogether. It is worth remembering that IBM was a fast follower in introducing its PCs. Some of the innovators (Apple, Tandy) survived in one form or another and some did not (Osborne).

Competition is what makes a market economy function as part of a just society and its absence, in the form of monopoly, also eliminates the major force toward improvement of products. Indeed, David Chappell, the author of a book on Microsoft's .NET initiative (Chappell, 2002), explicitly appeals to the importance of competition in assessing the status of various components of .NET. For example:

Those who think everyone should implement Java forget both the dangers of monopoly and the sloth which comes from having no competition. Having two powerful technology camps, each with a strong position, is the ideal world. ...In the end, competition benefits everyone. (p. 120)

Also, in discussing .NET My Services, Chappell looks to competition to insure that Microsoft will keep its promises about privacy: "Ultimately it's customers who will decide" (Chappell 2002, p. 309).

Unfortunately, in many instances, Microsoft has seemed to believe that competition is something to be stifled. When a market economy is combined with profit-maximizing capitalism, it is natural for organizations to want to restrict competition. Competition is necessary from the point of view of the consumer and from the point of view of a just society, not necessarily from the point of view of the firm. It is fine to say that consumers will vote with their dollars, but when there is only one candidate, talk of voting is meaningless. In a capitalist economy, the only meaningful restraint on competition to prevent monopolies from persisting is the government. Unfortunately, for the past few decades, United States' enforcement of antitrust laws has been fairly feeble.

In the case of Microsoft, antitrust investigations began as early as 1990, focusing initially on possible collusion between IBM and Microsoft on PC software.[7] After a series of Federal Trade Commission deadlocks on the issue, the Justice Department obtained a consent decree forbidding Microsoft from using its operating system to squelch competition. Microsoft basically did nothing significant toward obeying this consent decree. In 1995, Compaq wanted to bundle Netscape software rather than Microsoft's Internet Explorer with Windows. Microsoft refused to sell them Windows without Explorer. In 1997, the Justice Department demanded a $1 million per day fine from Microsoft for requiring Windows users to use Internet Explorer. Microsoft finally agreed to allow Explorer to be unbundled from Windows 95, but an appeals court in effect reversed the ruling.

In 1998, 20 states and the Justice Department filed an antitrust suit accusing Microsoft of abusing its market power to thwart competition. In 2001, after a rancorous trial and a failed attempt at mediation, the judge in the case ordered Microsoft to be broken into two companies. This decision was quickly reversed on appeal, and a change of administration resulted in the Justice Department's abandoning the proposed Microsoft breakup. Instead, a limited release of Windows source code was accepted as a settlement. Ten states refused to accept the settlement, but all have now settled. California, for example, accepted a large payment to be passed on to consumers. This settlement and most of the others do nothing whatever to ameliorate the problem. The European Union (EU) continues to pursue its own antitrust case against Microsoft. Interestingly enough, China was able to get Microsoft to release Windows source code to it, not for formal antitrust reasons, but just as a condition for Microsoft's entering the Chinese market.[8]

.NET My Services

I am reviewing this history to get a realistic picture of how Microsoft is likely to act in situations involving competitive advantage. Over and above the lessons to be drawn about the justice and monopoly, monopolistic practices sometimes do not even benefit the monopolist. Microsoft's .NET My Services provides server-located data and applications that place users at the mercy of Microsoft with respect to pricing and other policies. Chappell, in his *Understanding .NET* (2002), asks exactly this question: "Won't developers depending on .NET My Services be at the mercy of Microsoft?" (p. 317). What is to prevent Microsoft from raising its prices outrageously? He answers that competition will be enough to prevent this. Then, as an afterthought, he mentions that Microsoft "certainly has an advantage over any potential competitors… It can bundle .NET My Services into Windows." Of course it can, and it certainly has in the past, and with very limited incentive to stop doing so. And the results will be similar: monopoly control.

We can probably get a good idea of how things will go with .NET My Services from the past history of bundled software and Microsoft's use of its monopoly or near-monopoly position. Microsoft will probably not raise fees outrageously; any more that it does for MS Windows and MS Office. However, fees will probably be higher than they might have been in a more competitive environment. What is less encouraging is that Microsoft's priorities seem to be more to protect its profits than to improve its software. Besides a series of minimally improved upgrades, there have been no significant functional changes to MS Office since 1997. Michael Eisner, the Disney CEO, once railed against frequent Microsoft Windows upgrades and vowed to ignore the Windows 98 upgrade. I don't believe he was successful. Instead of functional improvements, many of the major efforts have been to curtail illegal use of unlicensed software.

But with .NET My Services bundled into Windows and hosted by Microsoft, we have a situation much less tolerable than with Office. If one is really betting one's business on Microsoft's hosting one's runtime application platform, there really needs to be some guarantee that one is in a true partnership with Microsoft. And this seems contrary to all its strategies. So Microsoft, with its history of anticompetitive practices, is not in a good position to market .NET My Services. It could split off the hosting portion of .NET My Services as a separate non-profit corporation, to be run in a hands-off manner from Microsoft. The tricky part would be guaranteeing true hands-off status. A government agency might be a better choice, but there is no real history of successful public/private mixed corporations in the U.S. as there is, for example, in Singapore.[9] There are a number of issues that would need to be faced: How much of .NET would have to be given to the new corporation? Would the new corporation control further development of .NET My Services? If not, how could it avoid remaining in captivity to Microsoft? The real problem may ultimately be that Microsoft's anticompetitive and monopolistic strategies may actually be incompatible with the growth and deployment of .NET My Services.

Positive Functions of Monopoly

It is sometimes claimed that Microsoft's near-monopoly over PC operating systems and Office applications is really a good thing, because there are uniform universal standards for these items.[10] There are natural monopolies such as utilities, normally cases where the infrastructure is expensive and duplicating it would not be efficient. The same could be said for operating systems—they have expensive infrastructures and duplicating them would not be as efficient.

The claims for monopoly over competition seem rather weak in this case. Monopoly means not having to answer to competitive forces, and often enough Windows' standards seem more a matter of satisfying Microsoft marketing needs than user needs. The Windows operating systems seems to be an example of what is called *bricolage*, using a heterogeneous collection of parts put together without benefit of a unifying conception (Levi-Strauss, 1966). One consequence is a security system with lots of holes. Others include an apparent weakening of innovation. *Business Week* describes Microsoft as a "company in midlife crisis" (Green 2004). Apparently Microsoft has begun to believe its own marketing, that innovation is critical. And it seems to be unable to deliver. The new version of Windows, due in 2006, has lost many new features, but will have a new user interface, making it easier to store nontext files such as songs and pictures, and improved connectivity with other Microsoft products. Fortunately, a plan to make the new version of Office compatible with only the new operating system ran into technical difficulties; nothing very new, including leveraging its monopoly status at the expense of the consumer.

Ethical Principles Concerning Monopolies

There is nothing within the framework of a market economy itself to prevent monopolies, collusion, and price-fixing. Therefore, government regulation is needed to keep market economies efficient and just. In the United States, these regulations began with the Sherman Antitrust Act of 1890. The Act, based on the power of Congress to regulate interstate commerce, declared illegal every contract, trust, or conspiracy in restraint of interstate and foreign trade. A fine of $5,000 and imprisonment for one year were set as the maximum penalties for violating the Act. Because of court decisions, significant enforcement of the Act was delayed 14 years. (Generally, the Act has not been enforced under Republican administrations.) Subsequent additional government regulation included the Clayton Antitrust Act in 1914, enacted to supplement the Sherman Antitrust Act, and the establishment of the Federal Trade Commission (FTC), also in 1914. Later, supplementary acts to the Sherman Antitrust Act included the Robinson-Patman Act.[11]

In the United States, some conservative political groups promulgate the view that government is evil and private enterprise is necessarily good. These people are often powerful businessmen or supported by powerful businessmen. Obviously, the necessity for external institutions to enforce antitrust legislation conflicts with these views. Views regarding government and business as hostile adversaries are not very widespread outside the United States. Capitalist democracies such as Singapore and Japan regard government and business as partners in ensuring the well-being of the nation. And conversely, views of the absolute superiority of "free enterprise" have recently led to such disasters as the deregulation of the electricity market in California and the subsequent near-collapse of that state's economy. Where you have a natural monopoly, it is just as insane and inefficient to force a free market on it, as it is to force a monopoly on a natural free market, as was demonstrated by Communist regimes in the 20th century.

It is important, however, to note that conservatives are usually arguing from a base of the Principles of Justice—not only the Greatest Equal Freedom

Principle, but also the Difference Principle. The claim for free enterprise in the case of the California electricity market was not on the basis that power companies deserved freedom from government regulation, but that in this case a free market would be more efficient. The case very clearly underscores my point that markets require effective background regulation to work properly. In the case of the electric industry, which was not a natural competitive market, the effective regulation was difficult if not impossible to work out properly. There was neither a "visible hand" nor an "invisible hand" in sight and, as a result, everyone ultimately was worse off.

Even though mergers can often have the same anticompetitive effect, very often regulators seem only to demand the most minimal cosmetic competitive concessions when approving them. It is part of Microsoft's practice, for example, to buy up small, innovative companies and then abandon their innovations through neglect. This practice is obviously damaging to productivity and a violation of justice by making a number of groups less well off, probably including the worst-off group.

It is worth noting that conservative arguments also tacitly accept the Difference Principle as a basis for discussion of issues of the justice of economic distributions.[12] When more resources and wealth are allocated to those already quite well off, the conservative justification is that those people will invest and stimulate more economic growth. If this claim were true, the Difference Principle would be satisfied. For example, growth stimulation was one rationale for Bush's tax cuts of 2001. Even the conservative justification is not that people with more wealth and power have more influence and are able to get things their way. By anybody's standards, that would not be just.

Because of the critical role of a functioning market economy in a just society, legislation promoting competition and its enforcement takes on an ethical dimension. Likewise, the deliberate violation of antitrust legislation by corporations shows that they are not willing to accept the reasonable conditions for social cooperation required for a just and ethical society. When government is run by those who would prefer a social order based on power and influence to a social system based on freely cooperating citizens, much less can be done to enforce antitrust provisions.[13] As to what can be done in those circumstances, one should consider working through voting and political action to establish a government willing to enforce the Principles of Justice. In case one is impacted directly by monopolistic practices, the answer is different.

Ethical Consequences for Businesses and Individuals

A business (especially a small one), which has been unjustly harmed by monopolistic practices, can sue for redress. Two Web sites, Sherman.act Mall (www.lawmall.com/sherman.act/) and RPA Mall for Robinson-Patman Act (www.lawmall.com/rpa/) contain possible actionable grounds for violations of these two acts and assessments of one's chances of prevailing legally. Here are some samples:

- Independent businesses being put out of business by chain stores;
- Discriminatory pricing by suppliers to chains vs. independents;
- Cities and towns can sue on behalf of victimized businesses;
- State and local governments can sue to stop offshoring of jobs; and
- Abuses and discrimination of prosecutors in favor of big chains.

Again, because of the importance of monopolistic violation of the Principles of Justice, it is ethically important for victims of monopolistic practices to sue whenever there is a good chance of prevailing, and one can do so at not too great a cost to oneself.[14]

For an individual, the relevant ethical area is that of partial compliance. What is one ethically required to do against a monopolistic institution that has unjustly acquired immense wealth and power? By definition, if one is dealing with a monopoly, one has very little choice about the product or service in question. If one tries to run non-Microsoft office application software, the frequent result is lots of incompatibilities with Windows—because Microsoft did not release the Windows source code to non-Microsoft developers. It is not that there is *no* choice—one could install the non-Microsoft software and live with much more frequent crashes. Even without crashes, because Microsoft Office is a *de facto* standard, one reduces one's productivity by using anything else. Availability of trained personnel and communication with other organizations—and thus productivity—would be impaired by using non-Microsoft software.

So what would be the point of not using Microsoft software, both from an ethical point of view and a productivity point of view? From a productivity point of view, there would be absolutely no point. In this case, monopolistic practices have robbed us of possible better choices. From an ethical point of view, there also seems to be not much point. It is not ethically required for a person or business to shoot itself in the foot by installing non-Microsoft software. As was discussed in Chapter III, the key to a person's ethical obligations in an environment when others are not complying is this: If you are forced to do an otherwise unethical action because of unavoidable circumstances, demonstrate in what you do that there is a higher order principle you acknowledge, even though you are not following it in this case. Although it is not unethical to acquire Microsoft software, if one is convinced that its monopolistic behavior is a serious violation of the Principles of Justice, then this principle of demonstrating the higher level principle still applies.

However, there really does not seem much to do that is likely to be effective. In the case of Microsoft, complaining about Microsoft to one's friends and colleagues is not going to get you very far. Writing to elected representatives supporting antitrust action against Microsoft will help. Perhaps the most effective way is to develop what John Rawls calls a sense of justice and become willing to apply it in discussions of monopoly. Discussing the behavior of Microsoft and other monopolists against the background of the Principles of Justice is different from merely carping at behavior you don't like.[15]

IT and the Least Advantaged

So far I have considered the Difference Principle primarily as acting through a market economy as a background institution. Now I will consider directly how IT affects the well being of the least advantaged. There are two questions to consider: First, how does the use of IT by the least advantaged affect their life prospects? Second, how does the use of IT by other sectors of the economy contribute to the life prospects of the least advantaged?

The use (or lack of use) of IT by the least advantaged is partially addressed in discussions of what is called the Digital Divide (Divide Network, 2003):

There has always been a gap between those people and communities who can make effective use of information technology and those who cannot. Now, more than ever, unequal adoption of technology excludes many from reaping the fruits of the economy. We use the term "digital divide" to refer to this gap between those who can effectively use new information and communication tools, such as the Internet, and those who cannot.

One concern is that the more advantaged are getting the benefits of their own use of IT added to their previous advantages, whereas the least advantaged are not using IT and, therefore, are falling farther behind the more advantaged. One of the premises in this argument is that the use of IT leads to increases in personal productivity. For the present discussion, we will simply assume that this is so, that the use of IT, especially by the more advantaged, provides the advantaged with significant benefits. (Questions about IT productivity are discussed in Chapter XI, Valuing Information Technology.)

Attempts to ameliorate this problem are framed in terms of increasing the skills to use the technology rather than directly in terms of improvement of life prospects. From the point of view of justice, the assumption that an increase in IT skills will improve a person's ability to "reap the fruits of the economy," while reasonable, really needs to be examined through research. It could very well be that some improvements in IT skills are much better at improving the prospects of the less well off than other possible improvements. In any case, justice requires us to try to find out.

Another justice-related concern has to do with equality of opportunity, which is part of the first principle of justice of Greatest Equal Liberty: Society is to be arranged so that all members have the greatest equal liberty possible for all, including fair equality of opportunity (Rawls, 1999).

As of 2000, the U.S. Department of Commerce (2000) found that:

- 51% of all U.S. homes had a computer; 41.5% of all U.S. homes had Internet access.
- White (46.1%) and Asian American and Pacific Islander (56.8%) households continued to have Internet access at levels more than double those of Black (23.5%) and Hispanic (23.6%) households.
- 86.3% of households earning $75,000 and above per year had Internet access compared to 12.7% of households earning less than $15,000 per year.
- Nearly 65% of college graduates have home Internet access; only 11.7% of households headed by persons with less than a high school education have Internet access.

So there is no question that attempting to improve the IT skills of those who lack them, should also end up targeting the less well off. The question remains, though, about what priority the improvement in IT skills should have for improving the prospects of the less advantaged. By itself, fair equality of opportunity may justify efforts to ameliorate the Digital Divide. Insofar as it is difficult or impossible even to apply for higher status jobs without e-mail capability, justice would require making this capability available even to the least advantaged. (The Community Voice Mail project to be discussed shortly would be a step in this direction.)

The second question concerns the contribution of IT by other sectors of the economy to the life prospects of the least advantaged. In the United States, the homeless are a good candidate for least advantaged. So the question is: Are the homeless better off because of the use of IT in some sectors of the economy? We can assume that the use of IT has an impact for all groups, across the board. If government is internally more efficient because of IT, for example, in processing paperwork, that frees up resources to be used by anyone. The same applies if corporations or other organizations become more internally efficient because of IT. But none of that has a special impact on the homeless.

There are individual projects specifically targeting the homeless, such as Community Voice Mail, as described by Taglang (2001):

...in Community Voice Mail (CVM), a basic telecommunications system shared by an entire community of social services agencies to keep their phoneless and homeless clients connected to opportunity and support. CVM systems are stand-alone voice mail computers linked to telephone lines and Direct Inward Dials (DIDs) that are purchased from the phone company. The hundreds or thousands of DIDs correspond to voice mailboxes. A CVM Director distributes the voicemail boxes to hundreds of agencies across a community; the agencies in turn provide [homeless] clients with personalized, 7-digit phone numbers that can be accessed from any touch-tone phone, 24 hours a day.

This sort of project seems potentially a very valuable one for improving the prospects of those worst off.

Microsoft has also donated large amounts of money to projects attempting to ameliorate the Digital Divide. In 2003, China and Microsoft signed an agreement for Microsoft to provide hardware and software to rural Chinese areas (China, Microsoft..., 2003). In addition, in the period 1997-2000, Microsoft contributed more than $173 million to help provide technology access to students at all levels of education. Microsoft has provided ongoing support for Federal TRIO Programs of more than $30 million since 1996. (TRIO Programs help low-income Americans enter and graduate from college.) Microsoft has also provided grants to community colleges in New Mexico and black and Hispanic serving institutions to reach disadvantaged populations (Microsoft, 2000).

Thus, on the one hand, Microsoft illustrates sensitivity to the Principles of Justice in its efforts to promote equality of opportunity and the prospects of the least advantaged. One could observe that it is also increasing its customer base, but it could do this without explicitly focusing on the less advantaged. On the other hand, its attempts to stifle competition to serve its own interests work directly against the second Principle of Justice, and indeed sometimes against its own interests, as in the case of .NET My Services.

When we apply the Difference Principle and consider the IT usage of the least advantaged, we need to consider both the impact of their own usage as well as the indirect effects of increased productivity on their prospects. Even those less well off benefit from efficiency brought about by IT, even if they themselves do not use it. Wal-Mart's Guaranteed Low Price strategy benefits the less well off. Significant low-end consumer cost savings are brought about in part by IT-enabled efficiency in the supply chain.[16] But from the point of view of the Principles of Justice, increased IT skills for the less advantaged are not valuable just for their own sake. Increased skills must contribute either to the first Principle of Justice (Greatest Equal Liberty) by implementing fair equality of opportunity, or to the second Principle of Justice (Difference Principle) by improving the prospects of the least advantaged. Although it is very likely that increased IT skills for the less advantaged work to fulfill both principles, ethics and justice require us to maintain the proper focus in this area.

References

Chappell, D. C. (2002). *Understanding .NET*. Boston, MA: Addison-Wesley.

Chazewski, L. (1999). *Transitional properties of market-based economic systems.* Retrieved on June 19, 2004, from www.collegium.edu.pl/chajewski/ASA99-CHICAGO.htmDigital

Digital Divide Network Staff. (2003). *Digital divide basics.* Retrieved on June 19, 2004, from www.digitaldividenetwork.org

(2003). China, Microsoft to bridge "digital divide". *People's Daily Online.* Retrieved on June 19, 2004, from http://english.peopledaily.com.cn/

(2003). Microsoft opens Windows source code to China. *People's Daily Online.* March 17. Retrieved on June 19, 2004, from http://english.peopledaily.com.cn/

Green, J. (2004). Microsoft's midlife crisis. *Business Week,* April 19, pp. 88-98.

Levi-Strauss, C. (1966). *The savage mind.* Chicago, IL: University of Chicago Press.

Microsoft (2000). Microsoft answers call to bridge the "digital divide."

Redmond, Wash., February 1. Retrieved on June 19, 2004, from www.microsoft.com/press.

Rawls, J. (1999). *A theory of justice* (rev. ed.). Cambridge, MA: Harvard University Press.

Rawls, J. (2001). *Justice as fairness: A restatement.* Cambridge, MA: Harvard University Press.

Sen, A. (1999). *Development as freedom.* New York: Random House.

Taglang, K. (2001). A low-tech, low-cost tool for the homeless. Retrieved on June 19, 2004, from www.digitaldividenetwork.org/content/stories/

U.S. Department of Commerce (2000). *Falling through the Net.* Retrieved on June 19, 2004, from www.ntia.doc.gov/ntiahome/fttn00/confer

Endnotes

[1]   See Chapter II, A Background in Ethical Theory, "Right, Good, Just."

[2]   This condition is known by economists as *Pareto optimality.* For Rawls' discussion of Pareto optimality and the Difference Principle, see Rawls, (1999, Sections 12 and 13).

[3]   For a thorough discussion, see Sen (1999).

[4]   See Chapter II, A Background in Ethical Theory, "The Rational Basis of Ethics."

[5]   Some economists feel that the principles defining a market economy are themselves inconsistent. See Chazewski, L. (1999).

[6]   AD/cycle. See www.paullynch.org/ACN/ibmsaa.html; the latest Web reference to this item is 1997 or earlier. The latest new product connected with AD/Cycle seems to be around 1994.

[7]   For history of antitrust cases against Microsoft, see www.wired.com/news/antitrust/0,1551,35212,00.html

[8]   See "Microsoft Opens Windows source code to China." March 17, 2003. (http://english.peopledaily.com.cn/)

[9]   To provide similar infrastructure in the late 1980s, the Singapore government started a successful private company, Singapore Network Services.

[10]   My thanks to Bernard Johnson for this point.

[11]   Standard account of antitrust legislation from a number of Web Encyclopedias such as *Encarta*.

[12]   In Rawls' terminology (2001, Sec. 9), all parties accepting a principle as part of the framework of discussion make it part of *public reason*.

[13]   See also Chapter IX, Copyright and Piracy, "Corporations and Basic Liberties."

[14]   See Chapter II, A Background in Ethical Theory, "Rights, Duties, Obligations."

[15]   See also Chapter IX, Copyright and Piracy, "Corporations and Basic Liberties."

[16]   The savings may also be due to coerced pricing agreements with suppliers and substandard wages for employees. These issues will be considered in Chapter VI, Trust Issues in a Market Economy.

Chapter VI

Trust Issues in a Market Economy

In a competitive market economy, one is required to serve the interests of one's employer or corporation. As we saw in Chapter IV, Professional Duties, one can do this in several different roles: as an employee, as a manager, or as a consultant. In each of these roles, one's duties are often fairly clear. But there are a number of circumstances in which these duties are not the final word.

First, when corporate boundaries become blurred, as they are in contemporary supply-chain management, new ethical issues arise. In a traditional market situation, agreement with another company to charge a fixed amount is often collusion or price fixing and is both illegal and unethical. In a supply-chain context, agreements that a supplier charge a fixed amount are essential for vendor managed inventory. They are not illegal and not regarded as unethical. Similarly, outsourcing agreements require companies to be concerned for each other's well-being.

Second, when the behavior of the corporation itself is unethical, severe ethical conflicts can arise for managers who have a duty to do their best for the corporation. However, in the worst cases, personal ethics may dictate dismantling the corporation. These issues are another application of what we called *partial compliance* in Chapter III.

In this chapter, we will consider these issues from the point of view of ethical individuals working for corporations (or other organizations). Later, in Chapter IX, Copyright and Piracy, we will consider the ethical status of corporations themselves. Since corporations are not people, but are rather legal constructs with some (but not all) of the properties of people, their ethical status is not transparent.

Supply Chain Ethical Implications

A traditional supply chain involves three entities: a supplier, the business, and the customer. Traditionally, the business needs some supplies in order to produce or have available items it expects to sell to the customer. Traditionally, several suppliers compete to supply the business with these items, usually on the basis of price, availability, and/or quality. Price is usually negotiated and, although a good past history with a supplier may provide an advantage, the business regards itself as constrained only by its interests, not those of the supplier, in awarding subsequent orders. Indeed, in a competitive economy, the relation of the business to the supplier is parallel to the relation of the customer to the supplier. Customers, after all, have no obligation whatever to continue purchasing from the same business. It is up to the business to satisfy the needs of the customer better than other businesses. This normally involves doing better in competition on price, quality, and/or availability.

Ethics in the traditional situation mainly involves honesty on the part of the three parties involved in the supply chain. Misrepresenting the items on which one is competing is a traditional way of taking unfair advantage. If a supplier agrees to price or availability and then backs out, the ethical implications of reneging are clear. Similarly, if the business misrepresents quality to a customer, it is not likely to get repeat business. And if a customer fails to pay for merchandise obtained, the business has a number of legal and ethical options including repossession and arrest in serious cases.

IT has dramatically changed the way in which the supply chain can be managed. Wal-Mart in particular has been a leader in using IT to produce a more efficient supply chain (Foley & Mahmood, 1994). In effect, suppliers are chosen on a long-term basis and given the responsibility for managing the business' inventory of that item. The business forgoes the ability to obtain lower prices through negotiating on an order-by-order basis with different suppliers, but it directly negotiates its own inventory levels with the supplier, and the supplier competes long-term on being able to maintain those levels. Clearly, this sort of arrangement is advantageous with high- and steady-volume items. The business only has the inventory it needs to meet customer demands, and there is no slack caused by internal processing. The ability to have the right inventory levels may more than make up for small cost savings. And both supplier and business need to share an accurate and reliable inventory management system enabled by IT.

But the ethical situation changes. Rather than the supplier and the business pursuing their own interests and interacting through competition, a whole new layer of trust is added. The interests of the supplier become embedded in the interests of the business. Similarly, the interests of the business become embedded in the interests of the supplier. The supplier can no longer be concerned with maximizing quantity in its own interests—it must now be concerned directly with the proper inventory level for that item for the business. And the business must recognize that the supplier has forgone the chance for extra profit in the interests of a stable long-term arrangement.

The Efficient Consumer Response (ECR) model, developed in the 1990s and adopted by a number of supermarket chains, includes continuous replenishment (CRP) that requires supermarket and suppliers to enter into a long-term, net-price agreement. Only then is it possible for the supplier to manage store inventories directly. In the case of the Texas grocery chain H. E. Butt, it was necessary for both the chain and the suppliers participating in CRP to come to see the situation as potentially long-term win-win as opposed to short-term win-lose. A "non-antagonistic" mindset was required (Clark & Croson, 1995).

Some commentators argue that such arrangements are unlikely to be stable precisely because competitive profit maximization and mutual trust agreements are incompatible (Cox, 2004). Other commentators note that supply-chain efficiencies require the development of trust and that the requisite trust requires more than formal contract conditions, but is "developed on the basis of personal contacts and confidence in performance" (Claro & Claro, 2004, p. 411). A standard text on the management of IT notes that "for [successful sharing of corporate information], the partner firms must...have a high level of trust in each other" (Frenzel & Frenzel 2004, p. 503). I believe both set of commentators are pointing to the same difficulty: To obtain the cooperative benefit of supply-chain efficiency, both business and supplier have to acknowledge that coopera-tive benefits take priority over its own individual interests. The agreement is, in fact, an ethical one and is supported not by sanctions but by mutual recognition of a principle higher than individual interest. The problem is the stability of such an arrangement in the context of a profit-maximizing market economy. In the context of a competitive market economy, sanctions for violating such coop-erative agreements can only be supplied by market forces. In effect, if a supplier or the business is unhappy, it can take its business elsewhere. If the business or supplier is a corporation rather than an owner, any possible additional ethical persuasion is simply not available. Impact on the bottom line is the only relevant consideration. Therefore, long-term agreements with suppliers to manage inventory for mutual benefit need to be viewed cautiously, especially by the less powerful party in such agreements.

Wal-Mart's treatment of its suppliers is an interesting example. Wal-Mart is not only a corporation, it is by far the largest company on the planet. Its strategy is to compete entirely on the basis of low prices. (Wal-Mart's slogan is "Always Low Prices—Always"). So perhaps it is not surprising that it does not seem to have great concern for the well-being of its suppliers. As Charles Fishman (2003) points out, "... the real story of Wal-Mart ... is the pressure the biggest retailer relentlessly applies to its suppliers in the name of bringing us 'everyday low prices'" (p. 68-69). Fishman notes that Wal-Mart's 21,000 suppliers are constantly being required to lower their prices. He claims that, rather than being constrained by cooperative agreements with suppliers, Wal-Mart uses its size and power to achieve its own strategic ends. Wal-Mart spokesperson Melissa Berryhill disagrees: "The fact is Wal-Mart, perhaps like no other retailer, seeks to establish collaborative and mutually beneficial agreements with suppliers" (Fishman, 2003, p. 71). Because of its size, many suppliers have little choice but to deal with Wal-Mart on its own terms. Those terms are quite ethical in a traditional supplier context—it does not cheat suppliers, keeps its word, and pays bills promptly—but it is willing to drive such suppliers as Vlasic Pickles into bankruptcy and Huffy Bicycle into years of losses. Few suppliers are even willing to talk about their experience with Wal-Mart for fear of being frozen out. Wal-Mart has cashed in on additional threats such as moving production offshore, for example, to China (Fishman, 2003).

There is no question about the supply-chain efficiency Wal-Mart has been able to gain. Because of its size, it can set and enforce standards for suppliers, for example, requiring radio frequency identification (RFID) on products from all its suppliers by 2006. Again, in a vendor-managed inventory system, the additional burden of supplying RFID tags falls on suppliers, and many commentators feel it will be excessive (Handfield, 2004; Thomas, 2003). Rob Handfield (2004) notes that smaller suppliers still have little choice besides complying with Wal-Mart's requirement and recommends forming a supplier consortium to gain some bargaining power with Wal-Mart. He concludes, "Companies should worry less about the robustness of the technology and more about the motives and the impotency that it implies regarding a supplier's ability to control its own destiny" (Handfield, 2004, p. 2).

So what is the ethical status of Wal-Mart when it, in effect, "captures" suppliers under this arrangement and then proceeds to squeeze them on price? What becomes of the trust arrangement? Orson Welles' story of the frog and the scorpion comes to mind. A scorpion asked a frog to carry it across a river. The frog initially refused, noting that the scorpion would sting him. The scorpion pointed out that if he were to sting the frog in the middle of the river, they would both die—the frog from the sting, and the scorpion from drowning. Thus reassured, the frog let the scorpion get on his back and proceeded across the river. Halfway across, the frog felt the scorpion's sting. Dying, the frog said, "But what is the logic in this?" The scorpion replied, "This is my nature, and there is no logic in my nature" (Sarris, 1968, pp. 80-84). Wal-Mart is, of course, different from the scorpion in that it is in no danger of dying, but it is the same in having an unchanging nature—that nature is to follow its corporate strategy of minimizing prices.

To get a clear view of the ethics of this situation, we need to recognize that corporations are not ethical individuals. To the extent that these efficient supply-chain arrangements depend on trust, suppliers are in the same position as the frog. The nature of corporations, like the nature of scorpions, does not include trust. A properly functioning, for-profit corporation obeys the principle of maximizing shareholder profits. Period. This is not an ethical judgment about corporations, but rather an observation about their nature. To the extent that a supplier becomes the "captive" of a large corporation, there is no room for trust. Therefore, insofar as a supplier enters into a managed inventory agreement with a large corporation, it should not depend upon trust. Rather, the supplier must be able to enforce its side of the agreement without depending on the good will of the corporation.

Is it unethical for Wal-Mart to make agreements with its suppliers and then squeeze those suppliers? This is a misleading question because a corporation is not a person. It is a legal creation with some, but not all, of the properties of a person. In Chapter IX, Copyright and Piracy, I will consider constraints on corporations necessary because they are not people with ethical points of view. But here I want to consider the ethics of dealing with powerful entities that are not bound by personal ethical considerations.

Even though the corporation is a legal construct and thus cannot act either ethically or unethically, it is constructed out of individuals who can and should be ethical. So the appropriate way of conducting ethical dealings with corporations is through individuals. For small non-corporate business, there is no distinction: The (small) company is the owner or owners and these individuals are ethically responsible for what the company does.[1] But corporations are not individuals. Normally, corporations respond only to that which is "real" for them, namely, effects on profit and loss, thus the futility of issuing public statements about unethical corporate behavior. Corporations will not become ethical agents through discussion of any kind, because they cannot become individual ethical agents.

So too with Wal-Mart. Because the violation of trust involved is not an issue that is likely to garner wider public sympathy, the suppliers are on their own to negotiate conditions protecting their own interests. Perhaps a supplier's association parallel to a labor union might be in order, as Rob Handfield (2004) suggests. But such an association would likely be as much anathema to Wal-Mart as labor unions themselves. One of the things that corporations protect closely is their own power.

In the case of the "squeezed" suppliers for Wal-Mart, one way to avoid getting "squeezed" would be if it were possible not to let Wal-Mart gain the lion's share of one's business for a particular product line. Otherwise, demands for lower prices (a central part of Wal-Mart's strategy) will have to be agreed to. Interestingly enough, one media source reports that Wal-Mart has imposed a restriction on its suppliers that no more than 25% of their business be with Wal-Mart. Unfortunately, I have been unable to verify the reference. If this report is true, it would be ethically significant to know Wal-Mart's reasons for imposing the restriction.

It look as though, although Wal-Mart is sensitive to traditional ethical considerations in the supplier relationship—not cheating suppliers, keeping its word, paying bills promptly—it may not have fully recognized the ethical implications of converting the supply chain. In effect, it continues to treat suppliers as hands-off partners free to take their business elsewhere, when in fact a great deal of accommodation is required on the part of suppliers at their own expense. And Wal-Mart can continue to do so as long as it maintains its overwhelmingly dominant position in retailing.

Outsourcing Agreements

Outsourcing is another area in which separate companies need to acknowledge cooperative ties between themselves that transcend corporate interests. A typical long-term outsourcing agreement between a company and an outsourcer should be viewed, according to Applegate, Austin, and McFarlan (2003), as a strategic alliance. If the outsourcing deal is large and long-term, both parties need to be considerate of the other's long-term survival. For example, it may be possible for a company to get an outsourcer to agree to a price so low that the outsourcer's existence is threatened. The outsourcer may do this for competitive reasons or simply because of bad judgment. I recall an outsourcing deal in which we, the company, actually raised the outsourcer's bid because we thought it could not do the work and survive on the amount it was asking for. Our judgment was vindicated when the company went out of business before the deal was completed—it was clearly in the habit of seriously underbidding its work.

To a greater extent than with a supply-chain agreement, outsourcing agreements tend to come with attached mutual benefits and liabilities. It is important to distinguish between true outsourcing and subcontracting. According to Hancock and Oates (2001), in true outsourcing, it is not only the performance of some operation but responsibility and authority for the result and resources that are transferred. Typically, true outsourcing allows an organization to concentrate on its core competencies, what makes it money, rather than functions more peripheral to its business (Hancock & Oates, 2001). Because of the degree of integration of business processes in outsourcing, the business outsourcing its processes has to encourage the outsourcer to care about intangibles such as the well-being of the outsourced company. And of course, as in the example above, the outsourced company has to care about the well-being of the outsourcer.

The contrast with Wal-Mart and its suppliers is instructive. Because Wal-Mart is so dominant and has such a choice of suppliers, it does not need to worry about the continued existence or well-being of any of them. For Wal-Mart, suppliers constitute a competitive market. On the other hand, the suppliers are facing a monopolistic situation. If there were a genuine competitive market on both sides, the advantages of mutually beneficial cooperative agreements would more likely make themselves known.

Dealing Ethically with Corporations

So what is an individual to do when faced with a corporation conducting itself in a manner that would be unethical for an individual? The IT professional codes of ethics we examined in Chapter IV, Professional Duties, envision such possibilities: The ACM Code mentions the professional responsibility of assessing the social consequences of systems and possible whistle-blowing if management does not act to mitigate dangerous consequences. As we saw in our discussion of partial compliance in Chapter III, The Context of IT Ethical Issues, an individual's choice may be to comply with unethical orders or to quit. In that chapter, we discussed the ethical situation of the individual: There may be an opportunity to be a whistle-blower, but in spite of legal protections, this course of action usually costs the whistle-blower a fair amount. An individual may be fortunate enough to be able to cause the unethical behavior to change within the company without damaging his or her own prospects in the company. But one can hardly count on this happening.

What, then, are an individual's ethical obligations against a corporation that is acting contrary to ethical standards? The relevant ethical consideration is that, in theory, whatever the individual ultimately does, higher level principles have to be acknowledged by that action (Schultz, 1971).[2] The critical point is that even if reasons of interest make it difficult or impossible for an individual to do what he or she believes is ethical, it is still necessary for that individual to acknowledge his or her own ethical principles. It is easy to see why. If the fact that others are not behaving well was a sufficient reason for an individual not to behave well, the situation could never improve.

For example, if a corporation is making substandard hardware, an employee's ethical responsibilities differ depending on whether that employee has the ability to influence the strategy of the company. If so, then ethically the employee is required to use his or her influence. If, however, the company is unwilling to change (its market niche may be to produce substandard equipment until word gets around), the employee needs to consider leaving. If, for other reasons (e.g., family obligations), it is not possible for the employee to leave, he or she still needs to continue to make his or her position known. If the employee does not have influence, it may be harder make his or her position known, but ethically the employee still needs to try. The critical point is that ethically an individual must acknowledge his or her own ethical principles in what he or she does.

The trust situations we considered in this chapter involve mutually beneficial agreements or understandings between companies, rather than individuals. The ethical question is how to handle such situations when such agreements or understandings are violated. When there is a great disparity in the size and power of the two companies, as is the case with Wal-Mart and many of its suppliers, the ethical situation does not look that much different from an individual dealing with a company doing unethical things. As Fishman (2003) noted, Wal-Mart suppliers are even reticent to talk about their experience with Wal-Mart for fear of retribution. Just as with an individual, the disruption to one's business caused by making waves may be more than one is ethically required to do. In Chapter III, I called such actions *heroic,* meaning only that the action is more than what is ethically required.[3]

The ethical considerations are the same against a corporation that violates mutually beneficial cooperative agreements. The relevant ethical consideration is that, in theory, whatever a business ultimately does, higher level principles have to be acknowledged by what that business does (Schultz, 1971).[4] The critical point is that even if reasons of a company's interest make it difficult or impossible for the company to do what its owner believes is ethical, it is still necessary to acknowledge the owner's or the company's ethical principles in whatever action it takes. The reason continues to be that if the fact that other companies are not behaving well was a sufficient reason for a company not to behave well, the situation could never improve.

This is the relevant ethical theory. In practice, we have to recognize that a corporation is not an ethical individual but a legal construct with the goal of maximizing profits (for a for-profit corporation). So we cannot appeal to ethical principles we both share. In the case of long-term, mutually beneficial inventory arrangements or outsourcing arrangements, any additional stability can only come from appealing to the interests of the corporation—its own survival and its efficiency in producing more profits. Corporations are indeed sensitive to damage to their reputations. They usually want to be thought of as responsible citizens—not because they are participants in a social contract that they have a commitment to uphold, but because it is "good public relations" to do so. In this respect, corporations could be seen as at Kohlberg's (1976) Stage Three, Conformity, with a goal of "looking good" for others.[5] Extensive corporate philanthropy tends to be justified in this way, but it is ultimately for the sake of the bottom line. It is more important for corporations to be *seen* as caring and responsible, for example, for the environment, than for them to *be* caring and responsible. (Since they are not individuals, it is far from obvious that they actually *could* be caring or uncaring.) For the ethical individual, it does not matter whether anyone *knows* that he or she has done the right thing, but for the corporation, being *thought* to be ethical is the whole point.[6]

So appealing to possible damage to a corporation's reputation can be a good strategy. It may be that, if indeed Wal-Mart imposed a restriction on the percentage of business a supplier can do with them, it could be for reasons of reputation as well as possible impacts on the bottom line. However, we cannot expect corporations to behave exactly as ethical individuals would behave. So trust arrangements such as agreements for vendor managed inventor and outsourcing agreements have a built-in source of instability that, given current institutions, are simply part of the environment. Chapter IX, Copyright and Piracy, contains a more extensive discussion of the ethical status of corporations.

References

Applegate, L. M., Austin, R. D., & McFarlan, F. W. (2003). *Corporate information systems: Text and cases*. (6th ed.). New York: McGraw-Hill Irwin.

Clark, T. H., & Croson, D. C. (1995). H. E. Butt Grocery Company: A leader in ECR implementation. *Harvard Business School Case 196-061*. Boston, MA: Harvard Business School Publishing.

Claro, D. P., & Claro, P. B. (2004). Coordinating B2B cross-border supply chains: The case of the organic coffee industry. *Journal of Business & Industrial Marketing, 19*(6), 405-414.

Cox, A. (2004). Business relationship alignment: On the commensurability of value capture and mutuality in buyer and supplier exchange. *Supply Chain Management, 9*(5), 410-420.

Fishman, C. (2003). The Wal-Mart you don't know. *FastCompany, 77,* 68-78. Retrieved from www.fastcompany.com/magazine/77

Foley, S. & Mahmood, T. (1994). Wal-Mart Stores, Inc. *Harvard Business School Case 9-794-024.* Revised 1996. Boston, MA: Harvard Business School Publishing.

Frenzel, C.W., & Frenzel, J. C. (2004). *Management of information technology.* (4th ed.). Boston, MA: Course Technology.

Hancock, J., & Oates, S. (2001). Minding other people's business. *Supply Chain Management, 6*(2), 58-9.

Handfield, R. (2004). The RFID power play. *Supply Chain Resource Consortium, Hot Topics,* January. Raleigh, NC: North Carolina State University. Retrieved on September 6, 2004, from http://scrc.ncsu.edu/public/APICS/APICSjan04.html

Kohlberg, L. (1976). Moral stages and moralization. In T. Lickona (Ed.), *Moral development and behavior.* New York: Holt, Rinehart & Winston.

Plato. (360 BCE). *Republic.* Retrieved on May 10, 2004, from http://www.classics.mit.edu/Plato/republic.html

Sarris, A. (1968). *The American cinema.* New York: E.P. Dutton.

Schultz, R. (1971). Reasons to be moral. PhD Dissertation. Cambridge, MA: Harvard University.

Thomas, D. (2003). Wal-Mart's RFID plan too aggressive for suppliers. *ComputerWeekly.com,* July 1. Retrieved on September 6, 2004, from www.computerweekly. com/Home/Default.aspx

Endnotes

[1]   My thanks to Major Johnson for this point.

[2]   See Chapter II, A Background in Ethical Theory, "The Rational Basis of Ethics"

[3]   The precise term is *supererogatory*, "above what is asked."

[4]   See Chapter II, A Background in Ethical Theory, "The Rational Basis of Ethics"

5   See Chapter I, Ethical Issues in Information Technology, "Determining Right and Wrong."

6   This discussion echoes Plato's in the opening discussion of his *Republic*. (Plato. 360 BCE, 357a-367e)

Chapter VII

Offshoring as an Ethical Issue

Removal of jobs from one country to another to exploit lower paid workers tends to raise objections from those whose jobs are removed. However, historically, such jobs have tended to be low-wage, low-skill jobs, and the people holding them have typically not been able to mount effective resistance. Recently, highly skilled, highly paid IT jobs have begun to be exported from the United States, and although some of the questions raised are the same as for the earlier low-wage jobs, there are some different considerations.

What are the relevant ethical considerations involved in exporting jobs to exploit lower wages? In certain circumstances, there seems to be nothing wrong with this practice. If, for example, the currency exchange rate makes work done in the U.S. cheaper than work done in France, but otherwise the standards of living of the workers in the two countries are comparable, it is hard to see an ethical issue here. This seems to be a form of arbitrage on labor prices. "Arbitrage" is defined as buying the currently relatively low-priced commodity and selling the currently relatively high-priced commodity in the expectation that the market will correct one or both prices. In liquid markets, it serves a scavenger function to even out price disparities. For example, New York-London gold arbitrage is a recognized function performed by some firms. They buy the cheaper gold and sell it into the more expensive market. The net effect is to reduce or eliminate price disparities. It is a sort of benign communication function in a market economy, helping to even out prices consistently throughout markets.

Although offshoring has some of the features of arbitrage, it does not seem to have all the relevant features that make arbitrage a benign, healthy function of a market economy. The most important difference is that the "commodity" subject to arbitrage in offshoring is labor. In a true arbitrage situation, the commodity's location does not change the nature of the commodity, and this is why price differences in gold are simply fluctuations due to market functioning. But it makes a big difference where labor is located. The whole point of offshoring jobs is precisely that we don't want to move laborers from India or China to the United States, because then we would have to pay them prevailing U.S. wages. For offshoring to work, we must take advantage of a social context with prevailing lower wages. Offshoring is in fact a new ethical problem brought about by the availability-at-any-location feature of information technology. By the use of IT, we can take advantage of social contexts with prevailing lower wages when the relevant features of the job can be performed great distances away.

Professional Ethical Considerations

Offshoring is, first, a form of outsourcing and all the normal considerations that apply to outsourcing continue to apply when the outsourcee is a continent away. The ethical consideration here is due diligence on the part of IT professionals and managers to ensure that outsourcing will provide net benefits for the organization and its stakeholders. Of course the primary benefit for offshoring is to save personnel costs with at least equal quality of work. A major concern both with "regular" outsourcing and offshoring is the separability of offshored work. If constant feedback between the involved companies is needed, outsourcing is not a good option. It is also not appropriate to outsource strategic applications; the long-term reliability and quality of the outsourcer is still an important consideration; and oversight and project management need to remain with the outsourcing company (Applegate, Austin, & McFarlan, 2002). For offshoring, it is also important to consider whether English language skills or strong knowledge of American accounting practices are needed.

When these considerations are not taken into account, there are problems. Some sources estimate that fully half of offshore projects fail to deliver anticipated savings. Also, unless responses are highly structured, offshoring service calls can cost some companies customers (Ante, 2004). And maintaining U.S. levels of security on development projects can be difficult. Even with these difficulties, some companies continue to offshore because of the savings. But IT professional ethics requires one to be aware of the risks and to manage them appropriately.

Justice Between Societies

Over and above IT professional ethical considerations, the justice of the practice of offshoring is also an issue. If we want to determine the justice of the practice of offshoring, we cannot immediately apply Rawls' two Principles of Justice (Rawls, 1999a, 1999b). Under those principles, a set of institutions is just if it conforms to the Greatest Equal Liberty Principle and the Difference Principle (economic goods are distributed to make the worst-off as well off as possible). These principles would be freely chosen by the members of a given society to regulate their background political and social arrangements[1] (Rawls, 1999a). So these principles are agreed to as applying *within* a society whose members share cooperative benefits and cooperative burdens.

In international labor offshoring, economic benefits and burdens are experienced by different societies with different economic and political arrangements. Although it is claimed that offshoring will ultimately make everyone better off, a lot more discussion of how this will happen is necessary. Especially if we accept Rawls' social contract formulation of the Principles of Justice (1999a), we need to show how the principles governing international economics could be freely chosen by the participants and thus fall within the scope of just and ethical institutions.

In his later work *The Law of Peoples*, Rawls (1999b) considers how to extend the Principles of Justice to cover the international situation. There are several important differences. First, a social contract view of international justice requires principles of international justice to be chosen, not by the political officials of each nation or nation state, but by *peoples*. On a social contract view, members of a given social group are the source of state and national authority, not the other way around (Rawls, 1999b, pp. 25-27). Rawls notes that this view differs from most discussions of international law since the 1600s, although it is common in political rhetoric to appeal to the desires of "the American people" or "the people of Iraq" as a more fundamental level of political justification.

Rawls (1999b) constructs a second social contract to govern relations between peoples. He calls the principles chosen the Law of Peoples. He starts with a situation in which all societies have chosen the two Principles of Justice; in other words, all are free democratic societies. (It later turns out that other types of societies can be parties to the contract.) The basis for the second social contract is that the representatives of any society must be able to agree to principles without knowing how their society would be favored or disfavored by those principles. Once again, the agreement is fair, but this time it is between societies rather than individuals. The agreement sets up what Rawls calls the Society of Peoples.

Many principles that Rawls claims would be chosen to regulate relations between societies are analogous to principles that would be chosen by individuals to regulate their own societies. First, they honor human rights, respect each others freedom, and respect cooperative agreements made between them. Second, peoples do not intervene in each others affairs and only make war in self-defense. (These principles are parallel to the Greatest Equal Freedom Principle; Rawls, 1999a). Third, peoples have a duty to assist other people living under unfavorable conditions[2] (This principle is parallel to the Difference Principle; Rawls, 1999b). One (possibly surprising) agreement of the societies is not to be under the authority of one world government. Rawls (1999b) claims such a government would have to be either a despotism or an unstable empire torn by dissension.[3]

The Law of Peoples, as Rawls (1999b) formulates it, respects the integrity of individual societies. Not only is there to be no authority over all peoples; but the analogue of the Difference Principle, the duty to assist "burdened societies" (Rawls' term for people living under unfavorable conditions) is much more limited than the Difference Principle. One society is permitted to be a lot better off than another. The only duty is to help less fortunate societies to attain what is necessary to maintain a just democratic society. Justice between societies does not require redistribution to make the least well-off society as well off as possible (Rawls, 1999b, sections 15, 16).

Although the United States was a model for the Principles of Justice as a social contract of free and equal people within a particular society, it unfortunately fails as a model for the Law of Peoples as a social contract of free and equal societies. The United States has never endorsed the Universal Declaration of Human Rights and thus fails to acknowledge respect for human rights as a cornerstone for relations between nations (Chomsky, 1996). And, in the case of the recent war with Iraq, it has abandoned the principle of the Law of Peoples to wage war only when attacked.

The violation of this principle is relevant to the issue of offshoring, because however offshoring is to be justified, its justification requires the existence of cooperative international economic agreements that parties from different nations regard themselves as obligated to honor. If a nation like the U.S. regards itself as able to disregard accepted principles of international behavior because it is powerful enough to do so and not be concerned about the consequences, this is deeply destabilizing to the entire system of international cooperation. This consequence was immediately recognized by a number of U.S. business commentators, including the editors of *Business Week* (2003).

Since, at the time of this writing, the U.S. military adventure in Iraq looks to be no more successful than the earlier misguided U.S. military adventure in Vietnam, we can hope that the violation of the Law of Peoples will not soon be repeated, at least for reasons of self-interest. Thus the tendency to destabilize cooperative international agreements is hopefully not likely to increase. So I will leave aside this issue here and suppose that stable enforceable international agreements are possible between nations or peoples.

Rawls (1999a, 1999b) argues for another striking difference between the Principles of Justice and the Law of Peoples that is directly relevant to the offshoring discussion. Because peoples with many different cultures and traditions participate in the Society of Peoples, the representatives will not choose to trade off economic benefits and burdens between peoples. Rather, Rawls claims they would insist on equality between peoples. This striking claim goes right to the heart of the offshoring issue, so its justification is crucial. Rawls (1999b) says, "...no people organized by its government is prepared to count, *as a first principle,* the benefits for another people as outweighing the hardships imposed on itself" (p. 40, italics in original).

In other words, although we can have agreements between societies (and parties within those societies) that redistribute benefits and burdens, we must first be assured that the internal arrangements within those societies are just. It doesn't count toward the justice of institutions in the U.S. to point to our good work in Afghanistan. And, conversely, it doesn't ameliorate injustice in Afghanistan to point to our contribution to improving the lot of the least advantaged in the U.S. So the justice of transnational redistribution of benefits and burdens is necessarily a *secondary* matter, to be considered against a background of justly functioning institutions on the home front.

There is a parallel with how benefits and burdens are organized within a society. One of Rawls' (1999a, sections 27, 28) main objections to utilitarian theory is that it doesn't take individuals seriously enough. Utilitarianism is concerned with maximizing value or maximizing average value. It doesn't care very much about how any specific individuals (especially the worst-off) make out, as long as the overall sum is better.[4] Rawls' two Principles of Justice (1999a) are an alternative to utilitarianism; the Principles of Justice reflect care about what happens to the individual. So, similarly, a utilitarian-type approach to relations between societies would hold that as long as the net average value goes up, there is no further issue of justice. Rawls' Law of Peoples (1999b) is an alternative that cares about what happens in individual societies. Redistribution of benefits and burdens between societies, if extensive enough, can easily wreak havoc with the internal justice of a society.

This is especially true when utilitarian principles govern relations between societies. Once again, under utilitarian principles, a loss on one society can be outweighed by a gain in another. So the losing society can end up, on its own terms, much worse off. An example, discussed at the end of the next section, is corn production in the U.S. and Mexico after the North American Free Trade Agreement (NAFTA). Subsidized U.S. corn drove small Mexican corn producers out of business. Since we are separate societies, most out-of-work Mexicans who come to the U.S. to raise corn now shipped to Mexico often come as illegal aliens (Bensinger, 2003). Clearly issues of justice no longer stay neatly within the boundaries of societies.

The Justice of Offshoring

Once we are clear on the extension of Principles of Justice (Rawls, 1999a) to relations between societies, one point about offshoring becomes very clear. Offshoring cannot be justified only by showing that people in another society are better off because of it. For the practice to be just, it must be shown that members of the society losing positions are not being treated unjustly. I will now review some of the major positive arguments for the justice of offshoring and then consider how well they stack up against the Law of Peoples (Rawls, 1999b).

According to Thomas Donahue, President and CEO of the U.S. Chamber of Commerce, offshoring boosts our economy and companies create new jobs with the money they save (Konrad, 2004). This defense, if correct, would address the justice of offshoring by showing that those losing their jobs aren't harmed. But companies saving money from outsourcing are free to use the savings for whatever legal and ethical purposes they want—for extra dividends for their stockholders, extra health benefits for their remaining employees, higher compensation for their top executives, grants to hospitals or educational institutions, and so on. There is no direct requirement for them to create new jobs. Indeed, Marc Andreesen, the Netscape founder, although sympathetic to offshoring, remarks that believing new jobs will be created requires a "leap of faith" (Baker & Kripalani, 2004).

And, as Katharine Yung (2004) points out, replacement jobs tend to be lower wage service jobs. Adam Geller (2004) notes that a majority—53%—of new jobs are in restaurants or temp services or somewhat below-average-wage areas; average pay is about 12% less than older jobs with 14% less benefits.

But these kinds of concerns are dismissed as "whining" by Thomas Donahue of the U.S. Chamber of Commerce (Konrad, 2004). For him, as long as companies save money and the economy is uplifted, the practice is justified. He is joined by a number of commentators who advocate offshoring as another example of the economic benefits of free trade and open markets. These include Secretary of State Colin Powell (Weisman, 2004), Azim Premji, the CEO of Wipro, a leading Indian offshore service provider (Rai, 2004), and many IT startup venture investors including Accel (Ante & Hof, 2004).

The economist Paul Craig Roberts (2004), writing in *Business Week,* begins to articulate the difficulty: There is a difference between free trade of commodities and what he calls "labor arbitrage." Proponents of offshoring who think that the U.S. will benefit are assuming that labor will behave in the same way as commodities. Certainly this is true of Colin Powell; in speaking to the Indians, Powell urged them to open certain commodity markets as a quid pro quo for our allowing offshoring (Weisman, 2004). But Roberts points out that the economic doctrine of comparative advantage does not apply to labor, capital, and production technology.[5] In fact, we don't have any advantage—comparative or otherwise—over countries such as India and China, and there no reason to expect a balance of trade to materialize. The offshore countries ultimately get to keep everything. The final position outsourced could be the CEO.

Although this is somewhat speculative, there is some evidence that the decline of England as a major economic power from the 19th to the 20th Century was due to the English practice of offshoring increasingly complex jobs to the U.S.[6] More complex jobs represent more than labor that can be reproduced at any location; they are also a repository of skills available for innovation and new ventures. When this repository diminishes, so does the capacity for economic growth. So, from the point of view of the self-interest of a society, it should be a matter of concern that highly skilled technology jobs are being moved to other countries.

In addition to these self-interested considerations, there are considerations of justice. From the point of view of justice, employees are participants in a society and not just commodities.[7] But for now, we note that the world economy is currently not a cooperative venture on the part of those subject to it. At best, transnational organizations such as the World Trade Organization and the International Monetary Fund answer to the more powerful governments or to corporations, not to the peoples of the world.

The ethical problem with offshoring is that significant economic redistribution affecting the life prospects of citizen of multiple countries is being treated as if we were already part of a global society sharing benefits and burdens. This is simply not the case now. Instead, economic hardships are being imposed on people in some countries mainly because offshoring will improve the economic benefits of some companies.

Before we consider whether all of this would make sense in the context of a global society, let us look at the claim of *Wall Street Journal* writer Bob Davis that there is nothing that new in offshoring. In his article, "Finding Lessons of

Outsourcing in 4 Historical Tales," Davis (2004) instances the following four cases as being similar to offshoring:

1. The replacement of hand looms with mechanical looms in England in the early 1800s, which gave rise to the Luddite rebellion.

2. Repeal in 1845 of the Corn Laws that protected domestic English wheat production.

3. The automation of steel production in Homestead, PA, in the 1890s, which gave rise to worker/management conflict that resulted in a number of deaths in 1892.

4. Massive unskilled labor immigration to the U.S. from Europe between 1870 and 1910.

In Cases 1 and 3, the issue is framed as resistance to technological progress in productivity. With offshoring, no one is claiming that the offshored workers are markedly superior, either technologically or any other way except cost; therefore, the only possible similarity is resistance to management attempts to cut costs. Perhaps the assumption is that whatever management does to cut costs is just, but outside the *Wall Street Journal* community, this is not a very plausible assumption. Or perhaps the corporate ultimate goal of maximizing profits is seen to supersede ethical considerations.[8] In cases of productivity improvement, claims are often made about IT productivity resulting in better jobs within the society. For now, it is enough to note that no one is claiming that offshoring improves the domestic mix of jobs in any direct way. So Cases 1 and 3 are not parallel to the offshoring case.

Case 2, the British Corn Laws, is very much a protective tariff-type case, and including it as parallel to offshoring confirms that the author thinks that opposition to offshoring is equivalent to opposition to free trade and that labor is a commodity. The arrangement of tariffs and subsidies to position a nation's economy with respect to others is very much an internal economic issue and, as such, is subject to the Principles of Justice (Rawls, 1999a). There is no special reason to think that unregulated free trade between nations would produce the best results for all, any more than unregulated competition between companies would produce the best results for all. In neither case is the outcome likely to be just. In the case of competition between companies, there is a presumption that results compatible with justice will be produced as long as certain bad situations such as monopoly are avoided.[9] In the case of unregulated free trade, the interaction is much more complex, and each country needs to watch the impact on its economy and the justice of its internal institutions. Mexico, for example, probably should not have approved NAFTA without additional conditions. Allowing unregulated (subsidized) American corn access to Mexican markets rendered small Mexican corn farmers uncompetitive—about 400,000 of them left agriculture (Bensinger, 2003).[10] When these disenfranchised farmers attempt to emigrate to the country where their former earnings have gone, they can often do so only illegally. If one were serious about labor as a commodity, one should regard immigration laws as a violation of free trade.

The final case, Case 4, massive unskilled labor immigration from Europe to the U.S., is indeed one in which free trade held sway in immigration of cheap labor. Possibly relevant to offshoring, Davis (2004) points out the impact on the two labor markets. By increasing the U.S. labor force by 24% and decreasing the Irish labor force by 45% and the Italian labor force by 39%, U.S. wages dropped a significant amount and European wages increased a significant amount. Of course the obvious difference from offshoring is that, in this case, the labor actually emigrated and became part of American society, to share in its benefits and burdens and to be part of the same social contract as preexisting Americans. If we were to do something parallel now, it would be to allow massive Latin American immigration, or even to allow skilled technical workers emigration rights rather than temporary visas. We can, however, expect the effects on job markets to be the same, that is, increased wages in the offshore countries and decreased wages in the United States.

So none of these cases is parallel in relevant ways to offshoring. Treating the livelihood of one's fellow citizens as a commodity is hardly a contribution to a just society—nor even in the long-range interest of the society losing highly skilled jobs. The next question is whether it makes a difference if we consider offshoring in the context of a global economy or society rather than just in the context of the society losing jobs.

A Global Economy?

The preceding discussion makes it look as though the real conflict in the offshoring case is between stateless corporations attempting to cut costs and the peoples of various countries attempting to live in free and just societies. As we saw in Chapter V, Justice in a Market Economy, there is nothing in the structure of a market economy that can save it from its own defects; for example, the occasional intervention of an outside (usually governmental) force is necessary to deal with monopolies. But in the case of multinationals, there is no such force. Because of the lack of responsibility to the societies involved, offshoring of jobs currently has the same ethical structure as offshoring of tax liability.

Yet it may not be a good idea to have a single multinational force. Rawls (1999b), following Kant (1795), says that the peoples of the world, in formulating their background institutions, will decide not to have a world government. Rawls says that such a government would either be a despotism or a "fragile empire torn by dissension" (Rawls 1999b, p. 36). The background idea is that human beings are organized into separate societies in which political power is lodged.

But why couldn't we have a global society to which a global economy would be responsible? Could a global society be a natural evolution from independent villages to city-states to nations and then to a global society? The various enlightenment figures, including Hume (1739) and Kant (1795), who thought it was not possible, were writing in the second half of the 18th Century at just the time modern constitutional democracies were arising. Italy and Germany were still collections of small sovereign states. Almost all of the continents of North America, South America, and Africa, as well as large portions of Asia, were governed by colonial European powers. So in this context, a global society might seem unthinkable. But the central power of IT of connectivity, availability of information at any location, should make it no harder to administer a global society than it would be to administer a multinational corporation! Indeed the models could be the United States with its states with limited powers, and the emerging European Union. The ethical principles governing such a global economy would have to assume that human beings are not ultimately organized into political societies and, therefore, that there is an organization governed by higher ethical principles than the Law of Peoples (Rawls, 1999b). If so, a new original position needs to be constructed to account for these higher level principles.[11]

The individuals in the original position may still want justice administered on a less-than-global basis. But it does seem necessary to have some institution answering to the needs of the peoples of the planet in charge of regulating multinational corporations. In its absence, it is up to current governments, especially the more powerful ones, to make joint agreements to limit the excesses and injustices brought about by multinational corporations, and to make possible the sharing of benefits and burdens that would make it possible to consider offshoring as a just practice. Indeed, as we shall see in Chapter IX, Copyright and Piracy, the ethical status of corporations is problematic even within societies—it is not so much that corporations are bad or evil, but that their very structure makes them impervious to ethical considerations. Within just societies, there are some counterbalancing forces, but in the multinational community, even nation-states are often without much power.

As things are now, without a global society, the stated benefits of offshoring are very much utilitarian and thus don't respect persons or the justice of the societies involved. I need to emphasize that I am not asserting that offshoring is unjust. Rather, I am saying that what needs to be considered is its impact on justice in the different societies involved, rather than just utilitarian tradeoffs between societies. The economic impact on the societies losing jobs needs to be evaluated for its impact on the fulfillment of the Difference Principle (Rawls, 1999a).

Also, the impact on the justice of offshore societies needs to be considered as well. Utilitarian justifications ignore the crucial role of working toward just democratic societies. Improving economic well-being is possibly an indirect way to justice—but historically, major injustices, such as apartheid in South Africa, have been corrected only with severe economic pressure.[12] It is of some concern that China, a country with significant human rights deficits and departures from a society governed by the principle of Greatest Equal Freedom (Rawls, 1999a), is being treated as a full economic partner. Not only is there no incentive for China to change these practices, it may even come to have more power than the U.S. and even be able to impose its political culture on us. On the other hand, it could be argued that China is a society that is establishing the economic foundations for a society that can adopt the freedoms of the first Principle of Justice. Rawls (1999a) explicitly mentions the possibility of social circumstances not allowing establishment of the basic rights, but does state that any restriction of the basic rights of the first Principle of Justice is justified only when the restriction is necessary to prepare for its own removal. Currently, however, this does not seem to be how the Chinese leadership is thinking of its situation.

If we actually work out an arrangement for a global society with power over economic issues, then it may be possible to show that international labor offshoring is indeed just by considering the well-being of all involved as part of one economic system. In those circumstances, raising the well-being of a programmer in India may be just even though the well-being of an American is consequently reduced, because we are all part of one economic system sharing benefits and burdens. But this is not possible now.

Indeed, unless and until the entire world's economies are managed as a single economy, we can't directly trade off benefits and burdens between different societies. In current circumstances, the social cost to the United States of IT personnel losing skilled jobs needs to be compensated in some way. Perhaps there should be an incentive to corporations to provide job retraining to those losing jobs.[13] The savings from outsourcing are substantial so that giving departing workers substantial one-time retraining costs would not materially alter the economics of the situation.

We need to remember that justice is not the same as efficiency. Although efficiency is a component of justice, there are times when all the efficiency in the world or across the world will not justify bad treatment of individuals in our own society. On the other hand, competitive pressures need to be considered and do make a difference in the justice of the situation. We now turn to those issues.

Offshoring as a Competitive Necessity

Managers who are uneasy about the practice of offshoring may still feel that competition makes it necessary for them to offshore; otherwise, they may find themselves at a severe competitive disadvantage. In a competitive environment, one company may not be able to afford to behave ethically or even seriously consider behaving ethically when such behavior would produce a serious competitive disadvantage. This justification is mentioned frequently in discussions of offshoring. If all my competitors are reducing their costs by sending many of their IT services to India or China, I will be at a competitive disadvantage if I don't do so. In fact, I may even be failing to do my (ethical and professional) duty by my company and its stockholders or stakeholders.

To some extent, this is a general problem about the ethical status of corporations, which will be more fully discussed in Chapter IX, Copyright and Piracy. Corporations are legal constructs rather than individuals, with the directive (in for-profit corporations) to maximize shareholder value. And the people running the corporation currently have an employee or managerial duty to maximize profits. Michal Lerner (2000), a corporate critic, notes that "even the corporate executives with the highest level of spiritual sensitivity . . . have no choice but to accept corporate profits as the absolute bottom line" (p. 311). The corporation cannot become a more ethical *person,* because it is not an ethical person at all. So what is an individual to do, who has, on the one hand, ethical beliefs based on his role as a citizen in a just society and, on the other hand, conflicting directives based on his role as a manager or IT professional in a corporation?

In Chapter III, The Context for IT Ethical Issues, in the section on "Partial Compliance," we considered ethical obligations in an environment when others are not complying. The relevant ethical consideration here is that, whatever an individual ultimately does, the higher level principle has to be acknowledged in what that action (Schultz, 1971).[14] Even if the corporation is not an ethical individual, an individual as a manager is, and, therefore, embodies *both* points of view: Citizen concerned with justice and responsible corporate manager. So a manager may be in the unfortunate position of believing that offshoring is unjust as currently practiced and, at the same time, knowing that the corporation would be at a severe competitive disadvantage if it did not send jobs offshore. The critical point here is that even if reasons of interest make it difficult or impossible for a manager to do what he or she believes is ethical, it is still necessary to acknowledge his or her own (higher order) ethical principles in what he or she does.

As I first pointed out in Chapter III, if the fact that other people are not behaving well were a sufficient reason for an individual not to behave well, the situation could never improve. It may be foolhardy and completely unproductive to do the right thing in circumstances where ethical principles do not hold sway. But if so, such action is not an ethical requirement.

How do we acknowledge the higher order principle even when we can't fulfill it? This often requires considerable creativity. The suggestions I now make are based on those in the Chapter III section, "Partial Compliance." I will assume that corporations generally are not inclined to consider justice as well as efficiency. It is naïve to suppose that a discussion of Rawls' Principles of Justice (1999a) will cause a corporation like Accenture to morph into an ethical individual and modify its policies of offshoring tax liabilities. So the appropriate audience is probably those who recognize that considerations of justice are valid but still have managerial or professional responsibilities to maintain, such as competitive pressure to offshore.

Besides job retraining for those losing jobs and contribution to research for new jobs, I think it is important to exercise extra due diligence when offshoring jobs. It is always good policy for any kind of outsourcing to get as firm cost and benefit estimates as possible and to carefully vet the reliability and stability of the company to which jobs are being outsourced (Applegate, Austin, & McFarlan, 2003). But given the very likely disruptive effects of offshoring on a company's own personnel, it hardly makes sense to inflict those effects when there is not good reason to think the offshoring will succeed. In addition, potential difficulties caused by cultural differences need to be carefully assessed. Doing all this counts as professional ethical behavior in the context of competitive necessity.

An individual could also initiate support at the appropriate level for policy changes to make the practice of offshoring fairer, including lobbying. In general, corporations know that they will do better to obey the law, so changes in law are probably the best way to implement the ethical constraints on corporations that they are simply constitutionally incapable of imposing on themselves. Perhaps working toward more general ethical constraints on corporations may be the most effective way of demonstrating one's principles as a citizen in a just state.[15]

The belief that any kind of economic growth is self-justified seems to lie behind much of the discussion of offshoring as positive. In this and the preceding chapters, I have pointed out ways in which justice based on a social contract requires constraints on economic growth. These constraints insure that individuals are treated fairly by their societies. It is simply a mistake to think that economic growth taken by itself overrides the Principles of Justice.

References

Ante, S. E. (2004). Shifting work offshore? Outsourcer beware. *Business Week,* January 12, 36.

Ante, S. E., & Hof, R. D. (2004). Look who's going offshore. *Business Week,* May 17, 64.

Applegate, L. M., Austin, R. D., & McFarlan, F. W. (2003). *Corporate information systems: Text and cases.* New York: McGraw-Hill Irwin.

Baker, S., & Kripalani, M. (2004). Will outsourcing hurt America's supremacy? *Business Week,* January 20, 85-94.

Bensinger, K. (2003). Mexican corn comes a cropper. *Washington Times*, September 9, A1.

Chomsky, N. (1996). *Powers and prospects*. Boston, MA: South End Press.

Davis, B. (2004). Finding lessons of outsourcing in 4 historical tales. *Wall Street Journal,* March 29, A1.

Editors, *Business Week*. (2003). *Business Week*, April 14, 96.

Geller, A. (2004). How good are the new jobs? *San Fernando Valley Daily News,* August 1, B7.

Hume, D. (1739). *A treatise of human nature.* London: John Noon.

Kant, I. (1795). Perpetual peace. In H. Reiss (Ed.), *Kant's political writings* (pp. 93-130). Cambridge, England: Cambridge University Press.

Konrad, R. (2004). U.S. Chamber president promotes outsourcing. *San Fernando Valley Daily News,* July 1, A6.

Lerner, M. (2000). *Spirit matters.* Charlottesville, VA: Hampton Roads Publishing Co.

Mulligan, A. C., Hay, R., & Brewer, T. (2000). David Ricardo and comparative advantage. McMaster University, Archive for the History of Economic Thought. Retrieved on July 21, 2004, from http://iang.org/free_banking/david.html

Rai, S. (2004). An outsourcing giant fights back. *New York Times*, March 21, C1.

Rawls, J. (1999a). *A theory of justice*, (rev. ed.). Cambridge, MA: Harvard University Press.

Rawls, J. (1999b). *The law of peoples.* Cambridge, MA: Harvard University Press.

Reiss, H. (1970). *Kant's political writings.* Cambridge, England: Cambridge University Press.

Roberts, P. C. (2004). The harsh truth about outsourcing. *Business Week*, March 22, 48.

Schultz, R. (1971). Reasons to be moral. PhD Dissertation. Cambridge, MA: Harvard University.

Weisman, S. R. (2004). Powell defends outsourcing. *New York Times*, January 21, A7.

Yung, K. (2004). Can't we work this out? *Dallas Morning News,* August 2, C1.

Endnotes

1   More detail about these principles and their derivation appears in Chapter II, A Background in Ethical Theory, "Justice."

2   In *Law of Peoples*, Rawls (1999b, pp.35-38) states eight principles. "No World State" is not itself regarded as a principle, and I have condensed a few others. The one omission I find striking is agreement that there be a mechanism for dealing with violations of the principles.

3   Rawls attributes this point to Kant (1795).

4   See Chapter II, A Background in Ethical Theory, "Theories of Right: Intuitionist vs. End-Based vs. Duty-Based."

5   The economist David Ricardo developed the economic theory of competitive advantage in the early 19th Century. See Mulligan, Hay, & Brewer (2000).

6   Personal communication from Bradley Zucker.

7   Treating labor as just another commodity also reveals a tendency central to modern technology that will be discussed at length in Chapter XII, The Ultimate Value of Technology

8   The issue of the ethical status of corporations will be discussed fully in Chapter IX, Copyright and Piracy.

9   See Chapter V, Justice in a Market Economy.

10   In 1993, President Fox of Mexico proposed renegotiating these and other related agricultural issues.

11   One private/public consortium working on formulating principles for a just global society is the Global Governance Group at www.globalgov group.com, retrieved August 8, 2005.

12   Personal communication from Professor Wendell M. Dietrich.

13   Some policy discussions develop this possibility. See www.brookings.edu/ comm/policybriefs/pb132.htm.

14   See Chapter II, A Background in Ethical Theory, "The Rational Basis of Ethics."

15   See Chapter IX, Copyright and Piracy, "Corporations and Basic Liberties."

Section III

Ethics and IT Users

Chapter VIII

Privacy and Security

Privacy and security are the first topics involving the interface of the individual with information technology. The two topics of privacy and security are connected, because security is required to make privacy possible in an online world and privacy needs drive security requirements. I will first discuss ethical issues connected with privacy and then with security.

The questions raised concerning privacy are these: First, what is the ethical basis for the right to privacy? Second, in what way does IT impact or change the right to privacy? Some concerns about security are these: First, what are the ethical implications for security of the answers to these questions about privacy? At a minimum, we are surely ethically required to maintain security to meet the individual's right to privacy. Additionally, there are ethical requirements involving security that have bases other than privacy, for example, protection of underage children against exploitation on the Internet.[1]

Privacy

Privacy is a right of an individual. That is to say, it would be wrong for other individuals or institutions to compromise an individual's privacy.[2] An individual has this right independently of what is decided in any social contract establishing a just society. One looks in vain in Rawls' work on justice (1999; 2001) for an explicit discussion of the right of privacy, possibly because this right defines the limits of society's dominion over the individual. Human beings are not exhausted by their roles in society, no matter how just or well-ordered. In any social contract, the right to privacy would have to be agreed to as a constraint on any social contract, or so I believe.[3] Even though individuals do not consider their own particular interests in deciding on the Principles of Justice as a basis for cooperation, they still know that they will have ends to pursue and have a general idea of how lives are to be lived. They will want to keep private any part of their lives that need not be shared with others to ensure the success of social cooperation. I will call this the Right to Privacy: Each individual has the right to keep to himself or herself all matters not in the legitimate interest of the public.

The Right to Privacy in this form begins to appear in the United States in the last part of the 19th Century (Warren & Brandeis, 1890). The proliferation and improvement of communication technology begins to raise the issue in a serious way. Before the telegraph and telephone, the only ways of transmitting information over distances was to travel oneself to speak to another party or to write a physical message on paper to be delivered physically to some remote location. Under these circumstances, the only privacy issues would involve either violating some confidence in speaking or access to a written message by those not authorized to receive it, or actual physical intrusion into someone's personal space.

Warren and Brandeis begin their seminal 1890 discussion by noting that "in early times," the individual was legally protected from physical interference to life and property. They then outline how these liberties were extended. Protection against bodily injury was extended to protection against fear of such injury, and then, further, to offensive features of the environment (such as smoke, dust, and noise) and then, still further, to injury to reputation. Property rights were extended to intangible property, such as artworks, goodwill, and trade secrets. The authors see this as the natural development in civilization of greater sensitivity of feelings and attitudes.

According to Warren and Brandeis (1890), the contemporary right of privacy becomes necessary because of the growth of mechanical reproduction of information. They cite "the right to be left alone" by the media: "Gossip has become a trade...pursued with industry as well as effrontery" (p. 3). They discuss at length the bad social consequences of newspaper gossip, and they feel that law about defamation and slander does not properly protect individuals from the (different) harm done by violation of privacy. Instead, they turn to the right of individuals to determine the extent of publicity for their thoughts and actions. This right goes beyond protection of property and is based on the right to one's personality.

Yet, according to Warren and Brandeis (1890), there are legitimate public interests that override the Right to Privacy. The ethical issue is to provide guidelines for what legitimate public interests can override the Right to Privacy. Warren and Brandeis suggest the following: Individuals have the right to keep private any information not related to their performance of any public role, typically a role they have voluntarily assumed. Publication of otherwise private information is also permitted if necessary for ethical (or legal) reasons.[4]

Warren and Brandeis (1890) take great care to distinguish the Right to Privacy from superficially similar social and legal considerations. For them, the Right to Privacy is different from protection against slander and defamation—slander and defamation must be false and must injure a person's reputation to be ethically wrong and legally actionable. The harm caused by violation of the Right to Privacy is different—there is still a violation even if what is published is true and even if the person's reputation is not harmed. They often characterize the harm done as to a person's *feelings* and, in their hypothetical reconstruction of the history of the Right to Privacy, attribute attention to it as a matter of people's greater sensitivity. Unfortunately, putting the Right to Privacy on this basis makes it seem as though the Right to Privacy would not be necessary if people were somewhat tougher and more able to "suck it up

I think Warren and Brandeis (1890) are correct about the nature of the Right to Privacy but wrong about its basis. We need to go back to the original basis for using a social contract to derive ethical responsibilities. One of Rawls' (1999) main objections to utilitarianism is that it does not take individuals seriously enough.[5] If the social contract does not provide space for individuals' own lives, it is open to the same criticism. Rawls' first Principle of Justice, Greatest Equal Liberty, does specify individual liberties, but it justifies liberties solely on the basis of their contribution to the individual's ability to do his part in upholding a just society. We are social animals, and our acceptance of a social contract obligates us to spend a large proportion of our time and effort in upholding it. But that cannot mean that we are therefore to submerge our individuality and become, as it were, digits on the hand of a just society. Our purpose for considering social union was to enhance our individuality, not to submerge it; otherwise, there would be no point to even considering a social contract and the Principles of Justice that govern it. So the Right to Privacy must be a boundary condition on any social contract. More than being a matter of hurt feelings, this right goes to the core of who we are as human beings.

Technology and the Right to Privacy

As just noted, in 1890, Warren and Brandeis were already calling attention to the strains placed on the Right to Privacy by print and communication media. The advent of even more sophisticated and potentially intrusive communications technology obviously produces even more stress. When the Tampa, Florida, police have cameras surveilling every street in a neighborhood, privacy is lost. And information technology adds an entirely different range of cases of potential violation of the Right to Privacy. Privacy fears in the case of IT have to do with concentrating large amounts of private data about an individual and then giving them even more widespread distribution.

IT professional codes of ethics handle privacy differently. The Software Engineer's Code (SEC) merely mentions protecting privacy as a professional duty without any further comment (www.ieee.org). The Association of Information Technology Professionals (AITP) Code of Ethics (www.aitp.org) does call for protecting privacy but lumps it together with confidentiality. As discussed in Chapter IV, Professional Duties, obligations concerning confidentiality are typically based on agreements with organizations and vary from company to company. Also, the Right to Privacy is definitely a right belonging to individuals rather than corporations or organizations to which obligations of confidentiality are owed. . On the other hand, the Association for Computing Machinery (ACM) Code (www.acm.org/constitution/code.html) correctly distinguishes between ethical concerns about privacy and confidentiality, and specifies in some detail the actions needed to protect individual privacy. Confidentiality is correctly treated as a matter of keeping agreements, or an implicit agreement not to disclose information not directly related to one's duties for an organization.

The specific requirements necessary to maintain privacy mentioned in the ACM Code are these: Because of the IT-enabled ability to collect and exchange personal information on an unprecedented scale, there is increased potential for violating the Right to Privacy. IT professionals have the duty to maintain the integrity of this data, including its accuracy and protection from unauthorized access.[6] IT professionals also have the duty to ensure that individuals can review their personal information and correct inaccuracies. Only the necessary amount should be collected and should not be used without permission of the individual. Exceptions are for necessary system operation and maintenance, or when the information is evidence for violation of the law, organizational regulations, or professional ethical principles.[7]

The exceptions seem to be a natural IT extension of the exceptions mentioned by Warren and Brandeis (1890). And the duties seem to accurately reflect what is necessary to protect the digital shadow of the individual who has the Right to Privacy. Fundamentally, there is to be no access to the individual's digital shadow without his consent, and the individual must have access to it to insure its integrity.

We can now turn to issues concerning security with a clearer idea of what it is that security is ethically required to protect.

Security

Security always involves a trade-off. On the one hand, we want to prevent unauthorized access to some resource. On the other hand, whatever means we use to do this will result in more difficult access all the time, and occasionally make access very difficult. The key to my car prevents others from driving it off, but I must be careful not to lose the key. Also, the key mechanism itself can malfunction. Any security function involves exactly the same trade-offs. Does the extra effort to implement and maintain the security outweigh the bad consequences of living without security? In the case of high-valued and portable objects like automobiles, there is no question. But the trade-off question always needs to be answered. It is not very smart simply to add more security just for the sake of security.

These trade-offs generally do not involve ethical considerations.[8] It is just not in anyone's interest—IT professional, user, or organization—to have a security system that causes almost as many problems as what it is supposedly protecting against. There may perhaps be an ethical issue if a security system wrongly claims to provide certain protections, but one persistent feature of IT is the ability of hackers to discover or create holes in security systems. Therefore, a system may be sound when created, but vulnerable to attack later on through no fault of its designers. However, some systems do not seem to have been designed with reasonable care at the outset. Microsoft Windows systems, especially those based on NT, are designed with users having full access to all resources as a default, and then having to be explicitly restricted. This procedure seems to guarantee the continuing security holes that were demonstrated on a yearly basis at Comdex in Las Vegas.[9]

These issues—and the trade-offs—came up with some force in the summer of 2004 when Microsoft released its "Service Pack 2" to fix security problems with the Windows XP operating system. Some of the changes seem good, such as changing the default state of ports from open to closed. But others, such as an automatic firewall, have the potential to disable useful applications (Linn, 2004). In the past, some Microsoft security fixes have done just that. Automatic mass e-mail, the heart of spam as well as useful group e-mail distributions, became no longer automatic. Manual acknowledgment of each message was required, thus making the application useless for its original purpose. . It became harder to do spam with Microsoft software, but a valuable application was also lost.

I will leave aside the possibility of ethically culpable negligence in the construction of security systems and consider ethical issues involving security systems constructed in good faith. These ethical issues are: (1) A professional IT duty to build security systems of integrity and to respect security systems; and (2) a professional IT duty to build and maintain security systems that respect the individual's (user's) Right to Privacy and one's duties and obligations to one's employer and client. Fulfillment of these duties is the ethical minimum for a security system.

IT professionals have duties that come about because of the goal of their profession, irrespective of their duties or obligations to users, employers, or clients.[10] Security provisions have to be good enough to preserve the integrity of the system against damage, restricting access to system functions to qualified professionals. To develop and maintain these system integrity functions is a duty of the IT professional regardless of the wants of employer, manager, or user–or even regardless of obligations to these parties.

Since security features are derived from what is possible in an operating system, it is again a duty of an IT professional to assess the features of operating systems relevant to the circumstances and advocate (or prescribe, if possible) the operating system that best fits the circumstances. Integrity-preserving features need to be taken into account, but so also does the fit to the actual and projected applications of the systems, features that allow meeting duties and obligations to employers, clients, and users, and the privacy rights of anyone whose information is stored in the system.

Among currently popular operating systems, the matrix-type security built into Unix and Linux systems[11] seems more likely to preserve system integrity than the ad hoc security built into Windows systems. Perhaps this situation arose because Unix (and its derivative, Linux) were designed as multi-user systems, whereas Windows began life as a single-user operating system (MS-DOS) with added multi-user capabilities. The idea of a matrix-type system is that users (or groups of users) are assigned access rights to each and every object in the system. In Unix, each file (devices are treated as files) has an owner and a group, and rights can be assigned to these as well as to anyone on the system (Flynn & McIver-McHoes, 2001). The possible rights are read, write, and execute (abbreviated rwx); a dash (-) means no rights. Thus a (partial) security assignment in a Unix system might be as described in Table 1.

In Windows, security is a piecemeal affair. Particular applications (such as Microsoft Access) sometimes have their own security, but in any case, the presumption is that everyone has access rights to everything unless the appropriate administrator establishes something different. So from the point of view of professional duty, there is a presumption against Windows for security

Table 1. Example of a security assignment in a Unix system

file	owner	group	owner rights	group rights	genl rights
Printer	Sys admin	payroll	r w x	r w x	- - -
Payroll records	Dir hum res	payroll	r w x	r - x	- - -
backup	Sys admin	IT	r w x	r w x	r - -

reasons. Indeed, the same considerations make it harder for Windows to ensure meeting obligations of confidentiality to employers and clients, and duties to respect the Right to Privacy of the public.

Current Cases

I will now examine three current cases involving privacy and security to see how the issues just discussed play out in reality. They are: Privacy problems with the U.S. Defense Department's use of data mining to combat terrorism; concerns about privacy violations in the use of Radio Frequency Identification (RFID) devices; and privacy problems with consolidating medical information.

The Technology and Privacy Advisory Panel, appointed by U.S. Secretary of Defense Rumsfeld, issued a report in June 2004. It found serious privacy protection flaws in the Pentagon's Terrorism Awareness Program. That program is intended to catch terrorists before they strike by monitoring e-mail messages and databases of financial, medical, and travel information (Pear, 2004). Although the Panel thought searching digital data should be used to combat terrorism, it also thought privacy should be protected while doing so. Its recommendations were intended not only for the Pentagon's Terrorism Awareness Program, but also for privacy safeguards for IT use throughout government.

The Panel recommended that any government agency obtain approval from a special federal court "before engaging in data mining with personally identifiable information concerning U.S. persons" (Pear, 2004). Approval would be based on a showing that the information was needed to prevent or respond to terrorism. Emergencies would allow action without court approval, but such approval should be sought within 48 hours. The panel felt that the great risk without protection for privacy was the chilling of dissent, saying "those who trade liberty for safety, all too often achieve neither." It also made clear that its proposals would not apply to searches based on suspicions about particular individuals, and thus should not interfere unduly with the fight against terrorism.

The terrorism issue raises the trade-off between individual rights and security at a high-stakes level. If security against terrorism is framed as a battle against a shadowy and pervasive ideology that can show up unexpectedly like a disease, then individual rights will probably suffer. But terrorism is not a political ideology. There are no terrorist political parties, even in Iraq or Afghanistan. Rather, there are groups, often non-governmental, who adopt tactics that involve indiscriminate killing of civilians to demoralize. The groups we are concerned with now in the U.S. are militant Islamic anti-U.S. fundamentalists, most notably al-Qaeda, the group responsible for the September 11, 2001, attack on the World Trade Center. Obviously, we want to prevent further attacks by this and similar groups, but framing our purpose as a war against a tactic, terrorism, leads only to confusion and wasted effort. After all, historically, the U.S. has itself used terrorist tactics, explicitly in Vietnam, and also at the end of World War II in the firebombings of German cities such as Dresden and in the use of nuclear weapons against Hiroshima and Nagasaki. It is important to correctly identify the danger so as not to restrict civil liberties unnecessarily. The caution about security for the sake of security goes double here, because mistakes damage what we are trying to preserve.

The Technology and Privacy Advisory Panel identifies what we are trying to prevent as the chilling of dissent, thus linking it to freedom of thought, speech, and assembly. But, important as these freedoms are in maintaining our ability to function as citizens of a democracy, we have seen that the Right to Privacy has a deeper basis. Judicial review of government mining of private individual data will clearly help preserve the Right to Privacy, but that review should also be on the basis of preserving the Right to Privacy as developed in American legal tradition by the courts since Brandeis.

The issue is really not different in kind from usual attempts by law enforcement to improve its efforts by violating privacy rights. The September 11 attacks give us no more reason to weaken the Right to Privacy than any other criminal activity. Of course, law enforcement may be more successful if it has completely free access to all types of information about anyone, but this kind of access is the hallmark of totalitarian states; indeed, what defines totalitarianism is the enforcement of laws being more important than the rights of citizens.[12]

Our second case: Radio Frequency Identification (RFID) Devices have also become involved in disputes about privacy violations. RFID tags are essentially "smart" bar codes that transmit wireless signals. Their use is for inventory control in supply-chain contexts, as well as automatic toll collection. Utah has passed, and California is considering, legislation to require that RFID devices be deactivated before leaving the store. Privacy advocates are concerned about violation of the Right to Privacy, in the form of automatic tracking of all consumer purchases. Technologists are concerned that the growth of technology may be hampered. Dan Mullen, an RFID industry advocate, instances receipt-free product returns and item location for the handicapped (Claburn, 2004). This kind of dispute—between ethical considerations and the imperatives of technological progress—is very common. One side points to the violation of ethical principles; the other points to possible future benefits from ignoring the ethical principles. We are asked to trade off a major invasion of privacy for what amounts to paperwork reduction. Mentioning helping the handicapped seems to be just rhetoric, as is often the other popular technologist claim of new cures for diseases. There does not seem to be a compelling ethical reason to violate the Right to Privacy in this case, especially since there is not a good case that respecting the Right to Privacy will hamper the development of this technology. This kind of dispute will receive extended discussion in Chapter XII, The Ultimate Value of Technology, and Chapter XIII, The Ultimate Value of Information Technology.

Our third case: The goal of President Bush and 2004 Democratic presidential candidate John Kerry was to make medical records uniform and electronic. The major stumbling block is just the absence of standards to create records readable by all. Privacy is also seen as an obstacle, but not by everyone. Dr. Louise Liang, Senior VP of Kaiser Hospitals, contends that privacy protection will be a benefit of electronic records:

Electronic records safeguards for medical records are actually much more secure than old-fashioned paper records, which sit around on desks and on shelves, frankly, unsecured...You have no way of knowing who looked at a [paper] record. (McGee, 2004, p. 24)

Her claims are dubious. On the one hand, most desks and shelves in medical offices are not accessible to the general public or to government agencies. On the other hand, if records are digitized, it will take special legislation to insure that centralized medical information is not available. The potential detrimental uses of centralized medical information are great. Perhaps the problem is that you *will* have a very good idea of who will be looking at centralized medical information, almost certainly insurance companies. This is unlikely to be in the individual's favor. Note first that health may be the most important enabling value–we must have it to be able to do anything else. Note also that the insurance companies who control health care distribution in the United States have strong motivation to pay as little on claims as possible and pay as few claims as possible. The potential for a great deal of damage, not only to the Right to Privacy but to the ability of some to get adequate health care, is large. Without something other than a voluntary system run by health insurance companies to monitor possible abuses of a centralized medical records database, possible damage may even outweigh the clear benefits of uniform medical information.

References

Claburn, T. (2004). Privacy fears create roadblocks for RFID. *Information Week,* March 8, 979, 24-25.

Flynn, I. M., & McIver-McHoes, A. (2001). *Understanding operating systems* (3rd ed.). Boston, MA: Course Technology.

Linn, A. (2004). Defense mode. *San Fernando Valley Daily News,* July 2, C1.

McGee, M. K. (2004). High-tech cure. *Information Week,* May 3, 987, 22-24.

Pear, R. (2004). Panel urges new protection on federal data mining. *New York Times,* May 17, A13.

Rawls, J. (1999). *A theory of justice* (rev. ed.). Cambridge, MA: Harvard University Press.

Rawls, J. (2001). *Justice as fairness: A restatement.* Cambridge, MA: Harvard University Press.

Warren, S., & Brandeis, L. (1890). The right to privacy. *Harvard Law Review.* IV, 5, December 15.

Endnotes

[1]   Thanks to Frances O'Doy for pointing this out.

[2]   If someone has a right to do or have something, this means that it is wrong for others to prevent him from doing or having that thing. See Chapter II, A Background in Ethical Theory, "Rights, Duties, Obligations."

3   I believe the priority I assign to the Right to Privacy would be acceptable to Rawls. In his discussion of the basic liberties and their priorities in his later *Justice as Fairness: A Restatement,* he mentions "the liberty and integrity (physical and psychological) of the person" as necessary to properly guarantee all other basic liberties. (Rawls 2001, Sec. 32.4)

4   Warren and Brandeis add that it would be OK to publish such information in pursuit of one's own interests. This seems incorrect.

5   See Chapter II, A Background in Ethical Theory, "A Theory of Justice"; Chapter VII, Offshoring as an Ethical Issue, "Justice Between Societies."

6   'Duty' is the term I would use instead of their term 'responsibility'. See Chapter II, A Background in Ethical Theory, "Rights, Obligations, Duties."

7   I substitute "professional ethical principles" for "this code" because the ACM code is not now generally accepted. It is a very viable code, but without general acceptance, appeal to it is likely not be effective.

8   Although there could be a violation of professional IT duty involved if due diligence is not exercised in evaluating such trade-offs.

9   These demonstrations were not at the Microsoft pavilion, needless to say.

10   See Chapter IV, Professional Duties, beginning section and following section on "IT Professional Ethics."

11   Also present in older minicomputer and mainframe operating systems such as VAX-VMS and MVS.

12   The ethics of totalitarianism could therefore be thought of as Kohlberg's Stage Four of ethical development (Law and Order). See Chapter I, Ethical Issues in Information Technology, "Determining Right and Wrong."

Chapter IX

Copyright and Piracy

As I noted in Chapter II, information technology's basic feature of easy reproduction of digital information gives rise both to new benefits and to new ethical problems. Easy reproduction allows new—and sometimes unwelcome—ways of sharing material previously much harder to copy, such as digitized music and movies. Napster, based on the brilliant and revolutionary idea of distributed storage on millions of machines with no centralized profit-taking, was defeated by centralized profit-takers. Of course, there was also an issue of copyright violation. Currently, movie and music companies are aggressively pursuing digital copyright violators.

The response of the record and movie companies might have been different. The earlier technological advances of cassette audiotapes and VCRs facilitated copying music and video but did not elicit a wave of court cases against consumers. After an initial attempt to block any copying, the recording and movie industries realized that amateur copying was actually promoting sales. However, since the inception of Napster, music CD sales have gone down significantly. It is an open question whether copying or poor music quality is more responsible. Music commentators state that current industry producers have strong incentives to promote mediocre music in familiar genres.[1] An accompanying issue is control of channels of distribution to reduce competition against mediocre music.[2] In fact, much of what these companies now treat as piracy had always been considered "fair use" in other areas.[3]

As these issues show, although we can see clearly the facts about the IT situation, the ethical principles aren't clear. We see clearly that people can make digital copies at will, and that these copies can be available to anyone on a large network or the Internet. The ethical question is whether this is merely an extension of friends swapping copies (perfectly ethical) or whether it is an illegal (and unethical) violation of copyright. An entirely new method of sharing copies requires a rethinking of ethical principles. In this chapter, I will consider the ethical basis for copyright in property rights and ownership from the point of view of Rawls' (1999a) Principles of Justice. Then I will apply these results to the current issues involving digital copying.

The original stated purpose of copyright is to give the artist or creator of intellectual property the exclusive right to reproduce it, but not just for the artist or creator to be able to reap suitable rewards for his creation. Ultimately the existence of this right is to stimulate creativity. U.S. Supreme Court Justice Sandra Day O'Connor writes:

The primary objective of copyright is not to reward the labor of authors, but "To promote the Progress of Science and useful Arts." To this end, copyright assures authors the right to their original expression, but encourages others to build freely upon the ideas and information conveyed by a work. (Lewis 2001, p. 1)

The original intent of copyright has clearly been attenuated (and apparently distorted) in recent years as corporations come to hold copyrights and to use their influence in Congress to extend the copyright period indefinitely. The agreement by the U.S. in 1976 to abide by the (European) Berne Convention adds a conflicting principle. For the Berne Convention, the basis of copyright is an unlimited perpetual right to property, rather than the development of ideas.

The Digital Millennium Copyright Act of 1998 takes its cue from this departure from original U.S. principles and for the first time criminalizes "unauthorized access" to works that are published and sold.[4]

The recent Supreme Court case *Eldred vs. Ashcroft* upheld legislation by the late Sonny Bono extending copyrights for an additional 20 years.[5] The original copyright period of 14 years is now 70 years for individuals and 95 years from publication and 120 years from creation for corporations (Lewis 2001)! Since the greatest benefit from the extended copyright is enhanced corporate profits, any connection to stimulating creativity is indirect at best. Nonetheless, the ethical question concerns the justice of this situation. If contribution to corporate profits is a sufficient justification for having and enforcing a copyright, then recent prosecution of consumers for making digital copies is ethically entirely in order. If, however, there is not a basis in the Principles of Justice (Rawls, 1999a) for these restrictions, then there is an ethical basis for changing the legal environment, either through the courts or legislatures. However, as noted in Chapter II, in the section "Problems of Conflicting Principles and Priorities," the fact that a law is unjust does not give an individual the right to break or ignore it. Rather, attempts should be made to change the law.

Copyright is an instance of the basic kind of ethical principle we examined in Chapter II in the section "The Rational Basis of Ethics." Cooperative benefits occur if people don't break the social rule "not to copy" when it is to their own advantage. The question in the case of digital copying is how far the rule "not to copy" extends, and how to balance the property rights of the copyright owners with the public's right to free exchange of ideas as the basis for social progress.

Ownership and Justice

Property rights, like a market economy, are important features of a just society according to Rawls (2001). They are likely to be chosen as part of the basic structure of society determined by the social contract. A market economy is a very good candidate for a background economic institution in a just society because of its efficiency and lack of administrative overhead. It thus contributes to the well-being of everyone in the society, including the worst off.[6] Property rights have their place in a just society for two reasons: first, because social assets tend to deteriorate unless an agent is named to take responsibility for maintaining them; and second, because the right to personal property is a basic human right (Rawls, 1999b, pp. 8, 65). Personal property is a necessary material basis for full development as an individual in a just society and for self-respect (Rawls, 2001). But Rawls (2001) explicitly notes that two wider conceptions of property rights are not fundamental:

The right to private property in natural resources and means of production, including acquisition and bequest;

The equal right to participate in control of the means of production and of natural resources, assuming these are socially, rather than privately owned. (p. 114)

Rawls feels that these elaborations of property rights are not fundamental because they are not necessary for full development of individuals as citizens or for the development of self-respect. Also, the decision of what form of private property to adopt for a society (whether property-owning democracy or some form of liberal socialism) should be made with respect to the particular circumstances of the society, and thus can not be made as part of the general Principles of Justice (Rawls, 2001). Thus, for Rawls, neither the property rights distinctive of capitalism nor the property rights distinctive of socialism are fundamental.

The final piece of ethical theory needed for this topic is the ethical role of corporations. Rawls does not directly discuss corporations as part of a just society, but his discussion about a citizen's having a fair opportunity to exert political influence is relevant.

A corporation is a legal entity capable of acting in some respects as an individual, mainly in terms of property rights, legal liability, and political rights. Theoretically, corporations are created to serve the public benefit, and their trans-individual status allows then to function more efficiently, without constant shifting of property rights and responsibilities. (http://legal-dictionary.thefreedictionary.com/Corporation). A corporation is classed as private or public depending on whether stock is held by private individuals or not. Thus, a corporation, as a legal construct created for reasons of efficiency, clearly should not inherit all the rights of the individuals making it up. However, it should inherit rights when denying them would deny the rights of the individuals making up the corporation. And in cases where the only justification for corporate rights is the efficient operation of the corporation itself, the Principles of Justice require us to consider the impact of the corporation on the rights of individuals outside the corporation.

Thus, the claim that corporate holders of copyrights have the right to dispose of their intellectual property in any manner that they want—an "absolute" ownership right—is simply not supported by the Principles of Justice.[7] It would have to be shown that the individual's right to free expression is enhanced by absolute ownership rights of intellectual property, in general, or copyright extension, in particular. Since the opposite of enhancing free expression actually seems to be the result, there is a conflict here that is not easy to resolve.

I believe the Supreme Court Betamax decision of 1984 is the correct starting point.[8] The court held that noncommercial home use recording of material broadcast over the public airwaves was a fair use of copyrighted works and did not constitute copyright infringement. Further, makers of VCRs could not be held liable as contributory infringers, even if the home use of a VCR was considered an infringing use.

Fast forward 20 years and we find music and movie companies hard at work demonizing, prosecuting, and persecuting individuals for making copies for their own use. In the year before August 2004, the recording industry sued just under 4,000 individuals for downloading copyrighted music. Judge Nancy Gertner of Boston remarked that she had never before had a situation where "there are powerful plaintiffs and lawyers on one side and then a whole slew of ordinary people on the other side" (Bridis, 2004). People sued are forced to settle for amounts in the thousands because legal expenses for specialized entertainment or copyright lawyers would cost even more (Bridis, 2004). The Motion Picture Association of America (MPAA) announced in November 2004 that it would begin employing the same tactics, suing downloaders for amounts of $30,000 to $150,000. The MPAA apparently draws no distinction between downloading for personal use and downloading for resale (Hernandez, 2004).

The behavior of record and movie companies seems clearly legal but unethical. Those making and reselling copies of music and movies are correctly called pirates, and it is both legal and ethical for record and movie companies to pursue these people. But the spectacle of huge companies harassing their own customers in a very likely mistaken drive to increase profits is not heartening.[9]

Even worse, these companies are clearly set on stamping out digital copying wherever it may arise. The Recording Industry Association of America (RIAA) expressed concerns about the ability to copy music broadcast over Internet radio (Pondel, 2004). Movie studios have expressed concerns about TiVo to go, which allows users to transfer movies recorded on TiVo to other devices (Wong, 2004). On the other side, a California district court recently held that fileswapping service Grokster is not liable if its software is used to make illegal copies. Although this parallels the 1984 Supreme Court Betamax decision, legislation has been written by Senators Leahy and Hatch to make it a crime to "induce" people to violate copyright. The proposed Inducing Infringement of Copyright Act has the backing of most of the recording and music industry, as well as Microsoft. Opponents include Intel, Sun Microsystems, and Verizon Communications. These opponents are concerned that the act may stunt technological development (Woellert, 2004).

Although I don't think that furthering technological progress is, by itself, a good reason for not legalizing the record and movie companies' behavior, it is part of the ethical picture. What is critical is how the technology is being used. Recall Justice O'Connor's statement about the purpose of copyright, which was "to promote the Progress of Science and useful Arts and to encourage others to build freely upon the ideas and information conveyed by a work" (Lewis 2001, p. 1). Clearly digital copying helps greatly in disseminating intellectual property and, in this respect, furthers intellectual progress. Further, noncommercial possession of digital copies by individuals seems to be an important part of their right to personal property.

Of course, it has to be acknowledged that digital copying makes it more difficult for record and movie companies to collect revenues in the same ways they have been. But perhaps it would be better for them to be expending their resources on researching ways to profitability in a world that includes relatively free digital copying, than on trying to stamp it out. It is likely that any measures that are effective in making the world safe for a traditional revenue model for movies and music copies will also include measures that clearly violate the Greatest Equal Liberty Principle of Justice (Rawls, 1999a). For example, what I am writing here could quite conceivably fall afoul of the proposed bill by Senators Hatch and Leahy to make it a crime to "induce" people to violate copyright. It is hard to understand how a supposedly liberal senator like Patrick Leahy could even consider such a clear violation of Freedom of Speech—and for the sake of a property right that we saw as far from basic.

The conflict between the interests of corporations and individuals showed here needs further ethical discussion. After that discussion, I will return to the question of the individual's ethical response in the situation of digital copying of music and movies.

Corporations and Basic Liberties

In the United States, the basic liberties are mostly expressed in the Bill of Rights: Political liberty (the right to vote and hold office); freedom of speech and assembly; liberty of conscience and freedom of thought; freedom of the person (including freedom from oppression and physical assault); the right to hold property; and freedom from arbitrary arrest and seizure (Rawls, 1999a, section 11). These liberties are to be restricted only for the sake of another liberty. For example, freedom of speech can be restricted only when harm would result; the classic example is shouting "Fire!" in a crowded theater. Freedom of speech is thus restricted for the sake of another liberty, namely, freedom of the person, specifically, freedom from physical assault. In a just society, these liberties cannot be traded off for greater economic benefit. So claims that corporate profits would be reduced by expiration of copyright or by more extensive digital copying are not the last words on the issues, even when true. These issues of copyright have to do with the first Principle of Justice, which calls for greatest equal basic liberties for all.

All the basic liberties are necessary for people to have a chance of achieving their ends, whatever they are, in the context of a given society. Thus, in Rawls' view (1999a, section 821), people will be unwilling to trade off these liberties for the sake of economic advantage because, in the absence of the liberties, people would be unable to use economic advantage effectively to pursue their own conception of a good life.

There is another important way in which corporate activity impacts the basic liberties. Rawls (2001, p.177) mentions the Marxist objection that large accumulations of wealth prevent all citizens, whatever their social position, from being assured a fair opportunity to exert political influence. We can see an instance of this objection in the passage of the copyright extension, which was largely spearheaded by The Disney Company. It is almost openly acknowledged that legislators can be "bought" by campaign contributions by large donors. It is to the credit of some legislators (among them, John McCain,

Russell Feingold, and Thad Cochran) that they authored a bill attempting to reduce the impact of large campaign contributions in elections. Unfortunately, the implementation of the bill is under the direction of individuals not sympathetic to its aims and so it impact will largely be limited.[10]

The idea of Rawls' social contract is that each individual should have equal political influence. Rawls (1993) replies to the Marxist objection that accumulations of wealth and power, especially corporate wealth and power, prevent anything like equal political influence. His reply is that in a society governed by the Principles of Justice, the fair value of the political liberties is guaranteed. His example of how this would work is precisely through campaign finance reform, the prohibition of large contributions (Rawls, 1993, pp. 357-8). Yet this seems like a band-aid on what seems to me a much deeper problem of corporate power. This problem with corporation power is potentially much more serious than the monopoly problems discussed in Chapter V, Justice in a Market Economy. Those problems concern the Second Principle of Justice, which has to do with just distribution of economic goods. But when corporations are monopolies (or oligarchies) and those corporations are media companies, the ability to freely express political opinions may be severely restricted. Recent very disturbing examples include Disney's refusal to distribute the anti-Bush documentary *Fahrenheit 9/11*; and Warner Pictures refusal to distribute an anti-war documentary because it holds being anti-war to be a political position.

The underlying problem is that corporations are not individuals with an ethical point of view. They cannot be regarded as parties to the social contract. So it is no wonder that they so easily escape any kind of ethical accountability. A corporation is a legal construct. It is hard to see how it would even be possible to have a *legal* requirement for corporations to inherit *ethical* as well as *legal* properties from the individuals making them up. So we have the spectacle of tobacco corporations contributing predictably to the deaths of millions over the years—and still staying profitably in business even after paying millions in lawsuits.[11]

However, since corporations are human constructs, their basic structure can also be changed. Although we can not directly cause corporations to assume the ethical features of individuals, it is perfectly in order to impose conditions on their existence that prevent them from interfering with the workings of a just society expressed in the principles of justice. Indeed, given their currently unchecked power that will continue to erode the basic features of a just society, justice itself requires the adoption of some principles to bring corporations into line with the principles of justice. Here are some initial suggestions:

1. Instead of granting corporations effective immortality, make their continued existence dependent on an outside periodic ethical review. Perhaps there could be an initial 10-year review to establish the review, and after that every 20 years or even 50 years to reduce the administrative burden.

2. Adapt the Service Concepts of Alcoholics Anonymous to corporations. (Wilson, 1962) The success of Alcoholics Anonymous (AA) is due in large part to its innovative organizational structure. One feature is to avoid getting distracted by money issues. Many service organizations easily spend two-thirds of their time and energy in fundraising. By contrast, AA forbids accumulation of money. Even the international organization is required to give away any accumulation of funds over the amount of one year's operating expenses (Wilson, 1962, pp.62-66). As applied to corporations, setting a suitable accumulation limit not impacting the survival of the corporation (maybe two to three years' operating expenses depending on how cyclical profits are) and then *requiring* any excess to be distributed to the shareholders.

3. Current excessive top executive salaries need to be reduced for second-principle reasons. It is hard to see how multimillion dollar salaries contribute to the well-being of those worst off—in our society, the homeless, for example. Since proportional executive salaries are much lower in countries competitive with us economically, there seems to be no economic justification for these multimillion dollar salaries. Indeed, the large salaries are probably due to the fact that these executives set their own salaries. The rock star Simon Le Bon was once asked why rock stars always marry supermodels. He answered, "Why does a dog lick his balls? Because he can."[12] So some independent agency needs to be setting top executive salaries. (A board of directors could do this if it were truly independent.)

    Besides apparently unjust accumulations, the high salaries distort corporate leadership by placing emphasis on wealth and using power to acquire wealth. The types of people attracted to these positions and the kinds of decisions they make are more likely to be influenced by these considerations than ethical considerations, including serving the legitimate ends of the corporation itself.

Corporations are unique because they are legally individuals—and must be to fulfill their legal function. But they are not subject to the ethical considerations of individuals. For other groups such as governments and voluntary associations, ethical responsibility lies with the leaders of those organizations. And for governments, the Principles of Justice (Rawls, 1999a) provide a whole extra level of ethical constraints. However, for corporations, individual leaders are *legally protected* from being personally liable for the damages caused by their leadership. Therefore, the solution has to be a new set of principles for corporations that serve the function of providing ethical accountability.[13]

Michael Lerner (2000) proposes such a principle in what he calls a Social Responsibility Amendment, also calling for a 20-year ethical review of corporations. His review would be done by corporate officers, employees, and affected community members. He has a long ethical checklist for the corporation. The checklist reveals that Lerner is still thinking of the corporation as an ethical individual–it is required to show loyalty, be socially responsible, and so on. His checklist also makes no attempt to distinguish ethical *requirements* (duties and obligations) from items it might be *desirable* for corporations to do (e.g., encourage humility in its employees).[14] I think this is the wrong approach. The corporation cannot become a better *person* because it is not a person at all. And the people running it are currently constrained only by the directive to maximize profits. Lerner is clear that "even the corporate executives with the highest level of spiritual sensitivity...have no choice but to accept corporate profits as the absolute bottom line" (p. 311). But, rather than having each corporation required to adopt his extensive list of lofty spiritual goals, the first step is the minimal one of having corporations not act like sociopathic monsters: No killing people, no lying to cover up your mistakes, no thwarting the legitimate rights of your employees through union-busting, complying with accepted accounting standards for truthfulness in financial reporting. Even meeting these four requirements for a corporate ethical evaluation would be an enormous improvement in corporate behavior in the worst cases.

And further, since any principles for corporations are *political* principles instead of individual principles, we *don't* want them to embody what Rawls (1993) calls *comprehensive doctrines.*[15] In a constitutional democracy such as the United States, with freedom of opinion and religion, we can't expect agreement on doctrines about the ultimate nature of man or even moral doctrines. Many of Lerner's (2000) suggestions embody such comprehensive doctrines. As with the Principles of Justice generally, all we want and can expect is agreement on principles (legislation) providing a fair basis for cooperation, including corporations. The principles mentioned above could be a start.[16]

Ethical Response of the Individual

So what should an individual do in this situation? The laws and policies that allow record and movie companies to prosecute, harass, and stigmatize private individuals making copies for their own personal use are unjust. As I indicated before, that does not mean that it is OK to make digital copies at will. Rather, attempts should be made to change the laws and policies. If these attempts are unsuccessful, then some form of civil disobedience may be justified.[17] But for civil disobedience to be justified, one's actions have to be very clearly set up to demonstrate a point about justice.[18] For example, in the present case, if one decided to download music as an act of civil disobedience, one would first have to notify the record companies that one was doing so. Then, when they sued, one would have to willingly pay the penalty. Somehow, I don't think many people would want to do this. Of course, downloading music or movies and trying not to get caught has nothing to do with civil disobedience.

A better avenue for restoring justice in this area may be through the artists. Some filmmakers, notably Michael Moore, have publicly announced that anyone can freely copy some of their work—in Moore's case, his documentary film, *Fahrenheit 9/11*. And some music groups such as Team Love are using free downloads as a promotion device (Green, 2004). But there is no requirement on artists to reduce their income; rather, this is what we called a heroic action, one that would be good, but is not ethically required.

The greater influence and power of corporations is a stumbling block to attempts to change the law within the legal framework. We have seen how the lobbying power of Disney was instrumental in getting a major extension of the time of copyright. Political activists as disparate as Ralph Nader and Pat Buchanan and such mainstream magazines as *Business Week* have warned of the current dangers of too much corporate power. So there are active voices in this area. But it is clear that corporations will probably not willingly reduce their power, so the reforms in constraints on corporations I have suggested may not come to pass anytime soon. In the meantime, self-interest dictates not getting into trouble with the record and movie companies while keeping the dream of the original Napster alive.

References

Bridis, T. (2004). Downloaders hit hard with fines. *San Fernando Valley Daily News*, August 22, B3.

Green, H. (2004). Kissing off the big labels. *BusinessWeek*, September 6, 90-92.

Hernandez, G. (2004). Taking aim at film thieves. *San Fernando Valley Daily News,* November 5, B1.

Lewis, M. B. (2001). Music length protection. Retrieved on October 4, 2004, from http://www.serve.com/marbeth/music_length_protection.html

Lerner, M. (2000). *Spirit matters.* Charlottesville, VA: Hampton Roads Publishing Co.

Pondel, E. (2004). Piracy patrol eyes radio. *San Fernando Valley Daily News,* September 16, B1.

Rawls, J. (1993). *Political liberalism.* New York: Columbia University Press.

Rawls, J. (1999a). *A theory of justice* (rev. ed.). Cambridge, MA: Harvard University Press.

Rawls, J. (1999b). *The law of peoples.* Cambridge, MA: Harvard University Press.

Rawls, J. (2001). *Justice as fairness: A restatement.* Cambridge, MA: Harvard University Press.

Wilson, B. (1962). *Twelve concepts for world service.* (Rev. 1990-1991). New York: Alcoholics Anonymous World Services, Inc.

Woellert, L. (2004). Piracy wars: Hollywood turns its guns on tech. *BusinessWeek,* July 19, 45.

Wong, M. (2004). No-go for TiVo? Studios contest mobility plans. *San Fernando Valley Daily News,* July 23, A3.

Endnotes

1   *LA Weekly,* July 2004.

2   My thanks to Neil Anapol for this point.

3   Personal communication, Eric Eldred.

4   Personal communication, Eric Eldred.

5   I am indebted to Eric Eldred, the plaintiff in this case, for helpful comments both on the case and its context, as well as on the application of Rawls' Principles of Justice to these issues.

6   See Chapter V, Justice in a Market Economy, beginning of chapter.

7   Thus neither the Berne Convention nor many aspects of the Digital Millenium Copyright Act would be supported by the Principles of Justice.

8   U.S. Supreme Court *SONY CORP. v. UNIVERSAL CITY STUDIOS, INC.,* 464 U.S. 417 (1984) (FindLaw Legal News, http://news.findlaw.com)

9   The MPAA's justification for calling personal copying privacy is based entirely on loss of profits.

10 Opposition is often based on the fact that free speech rights would be abridged by contribution spending limitations. Rawls (1993), in discussing contribution spending limitations, simply says spending limits would not be an undue burden. It is interesting that both sides are appealing to the preservation of the basic liberties. Differences may be due to different ideas of how liberties should be balanced when they conflict or on the incorrect assumption that corporations are full ethical individuals entitled to liberties as well as specific legal rights.

11 Multinational corporations are also not bound by considerations of justice when they send jobs offshore.

12 Interview with Simon le Bon, *Vanity Fair,* December 2003.

13 Limited Partnerships and sole proprietorships can also behave unethically, but the problem of ethical responsibility is considerably more severe in the case of corporations.

14 My thanks to E. B. Gendel for calling Lerner's work to my attention.

15   See Chapter II, A Background in Ethical Theory, "Theory of Justice", and Rawls (1993), p. 13.

16   The problem of ethical constraints on multinational activity of corporations would not be directly addressed by these principles; review would still be within particular societies.

17   See Chapter II, A Background in Ethical Theory, "Problems of Conflicting Principles and Priorities."

18   See Rawls (1999a, Section 55, "Civil Disobedience").

Chapter X

E-Problems

In Chapter I, I observed that new uses of IT will be built on four basic features of information technology:

- *Speed* of information processing
- Unlimited size of information *storage* capacity
- *Availability* of information at any location (connectivity)
- Easy *reproduction* of digital information

These features combine in many different ways to produce the various applications of IT that give rise both to new benefits and to new ethical problems. But, just as new and unpredictable uses of information technology arise with some regularity, so do new and unpredictable ethical problems. I will define an *e-problem* as an ethical problem that arises as a result of one of the four features of IT listed above. In this chapter, I will examine five unexpected and difficult e-problems:

- **Sales Tax:** Should sales tax be collected on Web-based transactions? If so, where and by whose rules? If not, isn't this an unfair advantage for e-businesses?

- **Paperless Transactions:** How does eliminating paper affect those without computers, especially those less well-off? How does one establish trust and appropriate controls without a "paper trail"?

- **Fraudulent Copies:** With a decent printer, it is very easy to duplicate virtually any document or picture—with or without modifications. This also makes it easy to produce fraudulent pictures. It is easy also to produce seemingly authentic requests for confidential information.

- **Spam:** Should freedom of speech allow so much speech that speech in the form of e-mail is itself jeopardized?

- **Dating/Sex:** The Internet enables ready access to sexual partners and dating. Does IT (the Internet) add anything new from an ethical perspective?

Sales Tax

Should sales tax be collected on Web-based transactions? If so, where and by whose rules? If not, isn't this an unfair advantage for e-businesses? What makes this an e-problem is the IT property of connectivity—the availability of information at any location. Sales tax is collected by states, and each state sets its own percentage and its own list of what is taxable and what is not. The tax is collected on transactions done by businesses with a physical presence in that state. Two U.S. Supreme Court rulings (*National Bella Hess, Inc. vs. Dept. of Revenue of Illinois* in 1967 and *Quill Corp. vs. North Dakota* in 1992) found that it would be an excessive burden for mail-order (and now, Internet-based) companies to comply with 7,600 state and local tax codes and thus an unconstitutional restriction on interstate commerce. Thus, the Supreme Court's Sales Tax Locality Principle was established (Institute for Local Self-Reliance, 2004):

Only firms with a physical presence in the jurisdiction are required to collect that jurisdiction's sales taxes.

Also, some "click-and-mortar" retailers contend that their e-commerce operations are distinct legal entities unrelated to their stores. Their Internet outlets therefore lack a physical presence and are not required to collect sales taxes (Institute for Local Self-Reliance, 2004). But many, including, for example, Nordstrom's (www.Nordstrom.com), follow the Sales Tax Locality Principle:

Orders shipped to AZ, CA, CO, CT, FL, GA, HI, IA, ID, IL, IN, KS, MD, MI, MN, MO, NC, NJ, NV, NY, OH, PA, RI, TX, UT, VA or WA [states where Nordstrom's has physical facilities] will have all applicable local and state sales taxes added to your total order, and to your shipping charges where appropriate.

Some retailers who are required to collect sales taxes are attempting to change the situation. They have proposed a Federal Sales Tax Fairness Bill which would require all retailers to collect and remit sales taxes. Such a change would incur the previous Supreme Court objection unless sales tax codes were drastically streamlined. There is a separate proposal by the National Governor's Association (NGA) called the Streamlined Sales Tax Project (SSTP), for uniform sales tax rules and definitions (Institute for Local Self-Reliance, 2004). Unfortunately, under this proposal, different state and local governments will still be able to tax different items and at different rates. The only change will be a uniform list of types of taxable items and procedures for publicizing change. It is hard to see how the NGA's proposal would meet the Supreme Court's previous requirement of no excessive burden.

But the ethical question behind the e-problem is one of justice. We have seen before that the Supreme Court does not always make just decisions.[1] And so we can ask, is the practice of exempting businesses without a physical presence in the taxing jurisdiction, a just practice? And are the Supreme Court's grounds for exempting businesses correct from the point of view of justice, namely, the burden caused by having to comply with a huge number of changing rules promulgated by a huge number of jurisdictions?[2]

To begin the discussion, let us assume that the sales tax itself is a reasonably just institution. For various reasons, it may be the only way certain jurisdictions can obtain funds for activities belonging to a just society (police protection, health care, etc.), even though the tax is correctly described as "regressive" in taking a significantly greater share from lower income individuals. The more important consideration is that Internet business transactions simply do not take place at a few specific physical locations. The distinctive IT property of availability of information at any location transforms the ability to locate a sales transaction.

Mail-order (and phone-order) sales transactions still take place at particular physical locations. The selling organization has its operations at one place, and the customer is at another. But with IT, the various parts of a sales transaction can easily be scattered across not only many states but many countries. From the point of view of justice, the tax should be collected at the point where it supports the infrastructure needed for commercial transactions between seller and customer. And the seller should be responsible for knowing only the tax rules for the areas in which it does business (and, therefore, has some responsibility for contributing to the infrastructure needed for commerce). But it is different when the marketing is planned in San Francisco, and executed on a server in New Jersey, and the order information is taken from a customer in Iowa, and processed by someone in Ireland, and shipping is coordinated in Seattle for shipment from a warehouse in Colorado, and payments are processed in the Bahamas, and questions about the transaction are handled in Bangalore. Where is the physical presence of such a company? The Supreme Court's Sales Tax Location Principle no longer seems to apply.

The consideration of justice underlying the location of the collection of sales tax is helping to support the infrastructure of the location where you do business. So it seems very wrongheaded to attempt to extend traditional sales tax collection to e-businesses. There would be some justice in having a separate national (or even international) tax to help support the IT infrastructure.[3] But there is no requirement in a market economy to make life safe for brick-and-mortar companies. Within a market economy, competition should decide. There is no requirement of justice, and, indeed, it would be misuse of government power to use government redistributive power to make traditional businesses competitive. It would be just as inappropriate for the government to prevent airlines from charging less for e-tickets even though travel agents are put out of work. A certain amount of economic dislocation is part of the workings of a free market, and, as we noted in Chapter V, Justice in a Market Economy, a market economy is an important institution helping our society satisfy the Principles of Justice (Rawls, 1999).

Paperless Transactions

The speed, storage, and reproducibility features of IT produce strong reasons to eliminate or minimize the use of paper for many transactions. Two different types of ethical issues arise as a result. The first is along the lines of professional duty: How does one establish trust and appropriate controls without a "paper trail"? The second is a "digital divide" issue: How does eliminating paper affect those without computers, especially those less well-off? Some colleges only accept online applications. And only students with ready access to computers can avail themselves of online courses.[4]

As soon as a good deal of transaction and managerial information is electronic rather than paper-based, the nature of both internal and external auditing changes. The two traditional choices are: Auditing around the computer, and auditing through the computer. The first choice, auditing around the computer, focuses on (paper) output and input. It is not likely to be recommended these days, nor is it particularly ethical because it will not reveal defects caused by computer processing. The second choice, auditing through the computer, requires checking the actual processing done to produce the output. Typically, sample data is actually run through the system.

Thus, business systems that rely on IT rather than paper produce a change in the duties of auditors (including managers responsible for the accuracy of control reporting). It is the auditor's professional duty to be IT-literate enough to understand how the company's system functions and its potential for error. This can be a tall order. I recall some years ago a yearly gross profit report calculated in two different ways by two different departments, presumably from the same data. When there was a 50% discrepancy between the gross profits on the two reports covering the same period of time, management demanded an explanation. It turned out that one report was based on calculated report information stored by date in a small file, and the other recalculated raw transaction data between selected dates. From an integrity point of view, the first method was a no-no and was a legacy from a very primitive stage of the system. However, its results turned out to be correct. The theoretically sounder method had produced the wrong numbers because, quite independently, a chunk of transaction data had been archived because of disk space problems. Fortunately, these days, disk storage problems are rare, but the ability to diagnose problems caused by system design continues to be a professional duty of auditors.

The second ethical issue concerning the disappearance of paper is an issue of distributive justice—of the second Principle of Justice (Rawls, 1999). Are those worst off made better off because of the disappearance of paper? This is, as I noted, a "digital divide" type issue. As I noted in Chapter V, Justice in a Market Economy, justice—specifically the second Principle of Justice—requires more than people having equal access to computers. For the distribution of IT to be just, it must tend to improve the life prospects of those who are worst off.[5]

In the case of the reduction of paper, justice requires that something be done to ameliorate possible reduced access to paper when that makes a difference in the justice of the situation. For example, job applications and applications for admissions to college made paperless result in a significant reduction of equality of opportunity for those without access to computers. In some countries, such as Mexico, Internet cafes are so ubiquitous and so reasonable that there is no problem about access. But in the United States, Internet cafes are rare. Libraries and public schools tend to have computers accessible to those without the necessary funds to have their own computers, but it still needs to be clear that equality of opportunity is not diminished. In any case, making job or school applications paperless without considering the potential impact on equality of opportunity is clearly unjust.

Some of the same considerations apply to online classes offered by public universities. If access is limited to those better off in times when there is a shortage of classes, it is hard to justify offering online classes at the expense of those more available to all. However, the disadvantage may be offset if the school has sufficient computers available for students so that accessibility is not an issue. Again, justice requires that one take into account potential equality of opportunity problems when school resources can be accessed only over a computer.

Fraudulent Copies

With a decent printer, it is very easy to duplicate virtually any document or picture—with or without modifications. This also makes it easy to produce fraudulent pictures, and seemingly authentic requests for confidential information. This is a consequence of the easy reproduction feature of IT.

With the use of IT, an important segment of one's identity is digitized. This digital extension of one's personality can be vulnerable to theft and misuse. "Identity theft" is becoming a more frequent crime. Early versions involved simply obtaining credit card numbers from paper copies in the trash or duplicating the numbers when entered. Precautions against this kind of theft included never printing (or e-mailing) copies of the whole number. More recently, one fraudulent technique (dubbed "phishing") is to e-mail bogus requests for confirmation of account information. I personally regularly experience a clever version that contains the logo of my (major) bank and mimics an official announcement very well. The reason given for the need for verification was the prevalence of identity theft! Included was a request for a prompt response with the warning that otherwise accounts would be suspended. A secure server was used as well—most of the trappings of a legitimate request. A phone call to my bank confirmed that the request was fraudulent. An obvious background question is, "How did the mimics know to e-mail me?" As it turned out, they were probably just "fishing," and they got my e-mail address from one of a number of Web sites I used. This hypothesis was confirmed when I got similar requests from two other large banks where I did not have accounts.

Of course, there is no question about the ethical status of identity theft and bogus requests for confidential information. They are both highly unethical as well as illegal. So too would be doctoring pictures to lead to false conclusions, except in a fictional context. When ex-President Clinton appears with fictional characters in the film *Contact*, the context makes it clear that his presence is fictional (Zemeckis, 1997). Ethically more tricky uses of easy digital reproduction were discussed in the previous chapter, Chapter IX, Copyright and Piracy.

Spam

Many other problems about the misuse of e-mail are similar to the previous problem of fraudulent copies. They are not so much ethical problems as problems of enforcement. But "spam," that is, anonymous unsolicited e-mail, does raise questions about freedom of speech on the Internet. Spam has been compared to unsolicited advertising mail, but one obvious difference is the volume. Throwing away junk mail is a minor annoyance. Getting rid of spam is time-consuming. Another difference is content. I don't get junk mail saying:

Best Priiiices

Best Selectiooooooon

vigilantism cheesy pol tackle basso deign newscast berwick bohr yoder abrogate bottle atavism ensconce sidemen handmade scratch crystallite approval byroad bathurst dahlia anvil jubilee.

cucumber confine ostrander muong joliet peggy sheriff bergson hattie lobo mentor pushout ambition eavesdropping eocene islamic perpetual appreciable shutoff madras antoine hectic contour donaldson hirsute ndjamena atavism presto gerhardt ditzel pygmalion convertible grenade oyster sup.

That is the content of a spam e-mail recently received. Like a lot of spam I receive, it is totally pointless. It would be like receiving dozens of phone calls where the speaker on the other end produced meaningless gibberish. What this has to do with speech or commerce is beyond me.

I think the Right to Privacy has to have priority over unsolicited freedom of speech to be meaningful. The Right to Privacy was stated as follows:

Each individual has the right to keep to him- or herself all matters not in the legitimate interest of the public.

This should include whom one wishes to communicate with, unless there is a legitimate public interest. No legitimate public interest is served by receiving unsolicited communications, except communications from a legitimate authority. We should simply require all unsolicited e-mail messages to contain an opt-out address (this might be accomplished simply by prohibiting phony return addresses), with fines for violators who ignore opt-out requests and fines or shut-down for servers who persistently harbor violators.

All first-principle freedoms and rights are limited by each other–they can't all be exercised to the fullest extent without conflicting.[6] The classic example is shouting "Fire!" in a crowded theater. Freedom of speech is restricted for the sake of another liberty, specifically freedom from physical assault. In the case of spam, freedom of speech could be restricted for the sake of privacy, especially since there is no public interest in forcing an individual to deal with a communication he or she did not consent to be party to.

Dating/Sex

It is not immediately clear that the Internet has introduced any new ethical issues in the areas of dating and sex. The Internet enables ready access to sexual partners and dating. What is perhaps new is due to availability of information at any location. People in small towns and rural locations suddenly have the same availability of sexual partners as those in densely populated big cities. The other feature of e-mail and the Web that makes a difference for this issue is the lack of censorship on the Internet. In part, this is because of inherent Internet design features—no one has to go through a central computer to be on the Internet, and, thus, effective monitoring is impossible. China has attempted to censor the Internet, mainly preventing access to pages the government doesn't like. One censorship device, know as the Great Firewall of China, attempts to block certain proxy servers. By all accounts, the censorship has not been very effective and seems largely arbitrary (Wikipedia, 2004).

In its effects in this and related areas, IT (through the Internet) has been a powerful force in resuscitating the freedoms of the First Principle of Justice (Rawls, 1999). Privacy, freedom of speech, and freedom of association are enhanced by the ability to communicate freely with others at any location with a computer. The abuses of that freedom in sexual areas—notably child pornography and exploitation of children—seem well within the current capabilities of law enforcement to handle. And that is just as well, because, short of shutting down the Internet, there is not much more that can be done about it that is not already being done.

References

Institute for Local Self-Reliance. (2004). Internet sales tax fairness. *The New Rules Project*. Retrieved on October 10, 2004, from www.newrules.org

Rawls, J. (1999). *A theory of justice* (rev. ed.). Cambridge, MA: Harvard University Press.

Wikipedia. (2004). Censorship in China. Retrieved on October 10, 2004, from http://en.wikipedia.org/wiki/Internet_censorship_in_China

Zemeckis, R. (1997). *Contact*. Burbank, CA: Warner Bros.

Endnotes

1.   In *Eldred vs. Ashcroft* on copyright extension. See Chapter IX, Copyright and Piracy.

2.   Various states have added extra conditions: Arkansas allows taxing competitors of products sold in the state, whether they have a presence there or not (Institute for Local Self-Reliance, 2004).

3.   Possibly an EU-style value-added tax would be more appropriate as well as easier to administer for this purpose.

4.   My thanks to Sarah Mallery for calling my attention to these issues.

5.   The second Principle of Justice is the Difference Principle—that economic inequalities work to improve the lot of the worst off. See Chapter II, A Background in Ethical Theory, "Justice."

6.   The first Principle of Justice is the principle of Greatest Equal Freedom. See Chapter II, A Background in Ethical Theory, "Justice."

Section IV

Ultimate Questions

Chapter XI

Valuing Information Technology

Besides being of interest in its own right, the question of the value of information technology (IT) has ethical implications, primarily for policymakers and managers in organizations. IT professional duty and managerial duty require undertakings that have a reasonable expectation of improving the organization and its prospects. Since IT plays a complex role in providing benefits for an organization, and also since IT projects can fail in ways that have major negative impact on an organization, the valuation of IT impacts the ethical responsibilities of policymakers and managers.

In the late 1980s, a number of researchers set out to quantify the value added to an organization by computerization or automation (two terms commonly used in those days). To their surprise, they found no or comparatively little value added. This result became known as the "Productivity Paradox" (Brynjollfson, 1992; Loveman, 1988; Roach, 1991). The ensuing discussion continued through the 1990s and beyond. Whatever else the discussion accomplished, it showed the complexity of questions about the value of information technology.

There are cases in which IT has clearly added value to a particular organization at a particular time. It is also true that, in some cases, IT has added more than shareholder or monetary value so that from any social point of view, the result is positive. The World Wide Web is an example. The difficulty in assessing value comes when one tries to reach conclusions about the overall contribution of IT to the economy or to society. It is widely known that IT benefits are far from automatic and sometimes difficult or impossible to achieve. So, overall, do the benefits outweigh the costs? How do we go about answering this question? What are the appropriate points of view from which to determine value?[1]

The two main appropriate points of view are:

1.   The *user* point of view. The user is whoever employs the technology, whether an individual, organization, or organizational department.

2.   The *socioeconomic* point of view, which is the point of view of the society or economy, whatever promulgates overall economic policies.

From the *user* point of view, typical questions would be as follows:

•   **Individual:** Is it worth it for me to purchase this firewall software?

•   **Organization:** Should we install ERP software companywide? What are the benefits and liabilities for the organization? Is the investment worth it?

•   **Independent Department:** Should we switch our production software to another company's product? Again, what are the benefits and liabilities for the department? (In the background, there should be a procedure insuring that potential impacts for the rest of the organization are considered.)

For the *socioeconomic* point of view, the main question would be: What IT deployment policies would produce the best social and/or economic returns?

Obviously there are many types of benefits and liabilities to be considered. The history of discussion of the Productivity Paradox is largely concerned with just this issue, namely, the types of benefits and liabilities involved in valuing IT. So we will first review this history.

The Productivity Paradox, Original Version

The original research, done in the late 1980s and early 1990s, examined productivity changes in various sectors of the economy. Research by Roach (1991) indicated that output per manufacturing worker increased by 16.9% between 1970 and 1986, while output per "information worker" (i.e., white collar IT worker) *decreased* 6.6% per worker. Research by Loveman (1988) showed the contribution of IT capital to output over a five-year period was approximately zero. Morrison and Berndt (1990) found that every dollar spent on IT generated $0.80 on the margin, not a very encouraging return.

Brynjolfsson (1992), in his review of these and other studies, concluded that even if one could not conclude from these studies that IT had failed to contribute to productivity, it was a matter of some concern that the contribution of IT could not be unequivocally demonstrated after huge effort and large spending. He suggested four possible explanations for the nonappearance of an increase in productivity: mismeasurement (of outputs and inputs); lags (in learning and adaptation); redistribution (of IT benefits); and mismanagement.

Mismeasurement refers to output benefits or improved inputs. Brynjolfsson (1992) actually means benefits not captured (and maybe not capturable) by traditional measures.. But is very hard to see why any attention should be paid to benefits that do not impact the bottom line somewhere, at least in principle. For example, Brynjolfsson cites the convenience of 24-hour ATMs as an nonmeasurable benefit. But without some real effect somewhere, it is hard to believe the benefit really exists. Even if 24-hour ATMs have no effect on transaction volume, then there should be some impact on customer satisfaction reflected in numbers of customers. ATMs may rather be a case of what Brynjolfsson calls *redistribution*. There are first-mover competitive advantages (and benefits in new customers), but when everyone has them, there are no benefits directly attributable to this use of IT, any more than there are to having restrooms or electricity.

It can simply be an excuse to claim benefits are nonmeasurable when there are no measurable ones. It is true that it can sometimes be difficult to measure benefits. However, to say there is no payoff measurable in time or money is to invite suspicion that there is no real payoff—period! Some readers may remember the advent of CASE tools for software development in the late 1980s. Productivity studies concluded that these tools did not improve development time or expense, but that the "quality" of the software produced was better. If that quality does not pay off in time or money somewhere, somehow, it is irrelevant. Likewise, if IT improves the quality of work life, that should also pay off in terms of worker output, somehow, some way, and if not, the improvement in quality of work life is irrelevant.

So for *mismeasurement* to be a defense of the productivity of IT, it would have to be true that significantly more of IT's benefits occur in harder-to-measure or indirectly measurable areas, rather than, for example, in reduced cost or time of manufacturing output. But even if this were true—that IT benefits are inherently hard to measure—IT by its nature would still be a riskier investment simply because it is so hard to get a handle on the benefits and thus determine the value it adds.

Lags are time delays in realizing benefits. This certainly seems a plausible reason for apparent lack of productivity within an organization, but doesn't make much sense as an overall socioeconomic reason. Within an organization, there could easily be a two-to-three-year initial period of reduced benefits from an IT implementation, but after that initial period, the productivity should show up. So, overall, there should simply be a relatively short delay in realizing productivity. Lag could not be a reason for low socioeconomic productivity unless the learning curve (and delay of benefits) for IT is really 20+ years—the period of overall IT implementation in society. But if benefits are available only after a 20+-year delay, IT again sounds like a questionable investment.

Redistribution was mentioned just above and refers to a situation where whatever benefits IT realizes simply are offset somewhere else, and there is no net gain. Between 1990 and 1996 alone, $1.1 trillion was invested in IT hardware—but about 60% of that was just for updates (Roach, 1998). Competitive catch-up, as discussed above with ATMs, is a frequent source of redistribution because it is necessary for firms to stay at least even with the competition in their IT capability, even when there is no net benefit. Failure to do so often produces significant losses in customer business. So these are cases in which an organization may need to implement IT without concern for productivity return.

Mismanagement is definitely a way in which productivity fails to be realized. Whether it is responsible for the apparent overall social lack of productivity is not clear. Mismanagement must be a concern because of the high failure rate of IT implementations. The question that needs attention from a user point of view is how an organization is to measure the possibility of mismanagement and include it in its deliberations about IT projects.

So mismanagement, redistribution, and lags impact IT value from a user point of view. From a socioeconomic point of view, mismanagement and redistribution seem to be relevant. But also from a socioeconomic point of view, mismeasurement and lags seem to beg questions in accounting for IT productivity shortfalls.

Productivity from the Socioeconomic Point of View

The middle to late 1990s were a time of explosive growth of the Internet, culminating finally in the collapse of the Internet bubble in 2001. The period of the bubble was also a period of extravagant claims for IT and what was called the New Economy, including claims that the productivity so elusive in the early 1990s had finally surfaced in the form of dot.com applications (Helm, 1999). Needless to say, those claims lost credibility after the collapse, and it is still not that easy to sort out what the actual situation is with respect to IT productivity. More recently, the productivity gains in the U.S. from 1996 to 2004 have been attributed to IT. Michael J. Mandel (2004) estimated recently in *Business Week* that overall U.S. productivity had increased 2.7% per year over the past 10 years, "fueled by [information] technology" (p. 35).

The value of IT from the socioeconomic point of view is probably going to be difficult to decide. If so, the question is whether any conclusion about value will be useful for setting social and economic policy. If we consider Singapore in the late 1980s—a society that utilized IT policies to direct their growth—we find that what drove social policy were issues of first-mover competitive advantage as opposed to IT value assessments (King & Konsynski, 1990). It would place too much weight on our fragile ability to sort out the contribution of IT to overall productivity if we actually used value results from the socioeconomic point of view to determine policy. Rather, an indication that the socioeconomic contribution of IT is positive is reassuring, and it leaves us free to consider IT projects for ourselves and our organization. This now seems to be the case, although it is worth keeping an eye on the overall socioeconomic contribution as conditions change. From an ethical point of view, considerations of overall socioeconomic IT value do not justify an obligation to pursue IT development—nor do they justify an obligation *not* to pursue IT development.

The Value of IT from the User Point of View

Things are different from the user point of view, whether it is the point of view of the individual or the organization. The relevance of the productivity issue is, as we said, for decisions about specific IT projects or acquisitions. What is relevant here is the continuing high failure rate of IT projects. Back in the 1980s, estimates of the rate of failure of IT projects were about 60%, split between about 30% of projects that were simply not completed and another 30% of projects completed but unusable. In 1994, a survey of large IT projects revealed that more than half were over budget, and only 42% were substantially completed; less than 16% were completely successful (Standish Group, 1994). In 2000, only 28% of projects were completed successfully (Satzinger, Jackson, & Burd, 2004). The individual manager must ask, "How can we quantify this risk?" "What are the chances that the project we are considering won't pan out, or will require significantly more time and effort?" This is the real impact of the productivity debate for individual organizations. An ethical manager has the responsibility to take these risks into account.

IT theorists have addressed the issue of risk of project failure. For example, Henry Lucas, a professor at NYU, has written specifically about individual organizations and how they realize value from their IT. Lucas (1999) distinguishes several different types of projects that contribute differently to value:

- Infrastructure
- Mandated systems (by government)
- Competitive
- Strategic
- Transformational IT
- "No other way"
- Direct return
- Indirect return

Only the direct- and indirect-return types of projects immediately impact value and productivity. Although some of the other types of projects may have a productivity impact, it tends to be low, diffuse, and very difficult to quantify.

Thus, many projects cannot actually be justified by expected value, using tools such as Return on Investment (ROI). The alternative justification of all these types of projects is some variant of: the project is necessary for business survival. Clearly, in order to be able to assess any such claims of necessity, managers need to have a good idea of the strategic and tactical positions of the company.

For example, suppose the claim is made that a new fiber-optic cable backbone is needed for the company, on the grounds that it is essential infrastructure. It should be possible to show that present or future capacity needs outstrip the current infrastructure and require something like the proposed infrastructure upgrade. We are only guessing about capacity needs unless we can ground them in the company's strategic and tactical positions. And there is indeed value for the company in this infrastructure project, but the value in infrastructure is what we called an *enabling value*. Infrastructure is a precondition for any other kind of value to be created. For the individual, health is an enabling value, a precondition for an individual to be able to create any other values.[2] And just as for the individual, enabling values for an organization are literally priceless, normally not subject to trade-offs for other values.

Actually, only value for direct-return type projects is easy to estimate. Returns and costs can be measured up front, the applications are well structured, and there is a very high probability of obtaining return on investment. By contrast, for indirect-return type projects, although they yield value, returns can often not be quantified, predicted, or scheduled in advance. Lucas (1999) instances a FedEx Web package location service. Direct benefits include reduction in 800-number costs and the ability to use the same staff for more inquiries. Indirect benefits include increased customer loyalty. My previous comments on mismeasurement apply here: Such benefits must in *some* way affect the bottom line, and if the connection of benefits to the bottom line is too difficult to determine, it is hard to have much confidence in decisions based on them.

Earlier in the history of IT implementation, the value of IT projects was somewhat easier to measure. Most organizations began by automating backoffice accounting and inventory functions, and gains in speed and reliability of internal processing were easier to measure or estimate. When IT expanded in the organization and beyond the organization, productivity gains became more difficult to measure, in part because of the frequent strategic impact of these applications. And the infrastructure benefits of the increased integration of centralized databases and the Enterprise Resource Planning (ERP) software built on them add another layer of difficulty to the measurement of IT value.

Managerial Consequences

Regardless of the rationale for a project, whether expected net returns or strategic necessity, the likelihood of completing the project and achieving that goal is critical. Some estimate of the probability of a successful conclusion to the project is at least as important as any assessment of value. However, much depends on contingencies. So it is difficult to get a very precise idea of the probability of success or failure of a given project.

Lucas (1999) attributes great importance to probability estimates. He proposes what he calls the *IT Investment Equation,* which is (in nontechnical terms):

Probability of return on investment =

Probability of return for investment type x probability of successful completion of this application.

From Lucas' examples, however, it becomes clear that his probabilities are *subjective* probabilities in what the philosopher Max Black (1967) calls an "extreme" form; that is, the probabilities simply reflect an individual's intensity of confidence. Black points out that these intensities fluctuate too much to make them usable. Thus, Lucas (1999) obtains a 100% probability of successful completion of a given application by noting that "the IT staff thinks the package will be easy to implement and estimates a 100% chance of successful conversion." And a 50% probability of success of a budgeting system (project type) is based on the fact that "[the new application] has a nicer interface and better reports, but managers could not honestly say the system will help them make more money" (Lucas, 1999, p. 38).

It seems plausible to suggest that overall likelihood of return on investment is a function of probability of success for that type of project combined with probability of project success. But it is very hard to have much management confidence in probability numbers arrived at in the method used by Lucas (1999). An alternative way of handling project risk, the risk assessment model developed at the Harvard Business School (Applegate, Austin, & McFarlan, 2003), has instead three risk categories: low risk, medium risk, and high risk.

Given the amount of subjective variation involved, it doesn't seem that a more fine-grained classification would be very trustworthy.

On Lucas' model (1999), probability of success for project type could perhaps be established with some degree of objectivity. *Objective* probability is simply frequency, so the objective probability of success of a project type would be the number of successes divided by the number of projects of that type. Of course, difficulties will arise in determining relevant project types, in making sure a project was correctly classified as of that type, and then in getting a representative sample. However, this might very well be a useful research project.

As far as probability of success of project completion goes, the Harvard Business School risk assessment model may be somewhat more useful (Applegate et al., 2003). The model includes two types of risk assessment, *portfolio risk* and *project risk*. A *portfolio* is the mix of projects an organization is implementing. Applegate et al. correctly point out that organizations in some cases *should* undertake some risky projects. Probably no organization should undertake only risky projects, but if an organization's strategy includes developing cutting-edge IT products, it *must* have some risky projects in order to pursue that strategy. *Portfolio risk*, the risk characteristics of the organization's mix of projects, is determined by a management decision about the strategic appropriateness of pursuing a given mix of projects, each with its own project risk. Factors influencing the appropriateness of including more risky projects in the portfolio are greater IT development competence and experience, as well as the strategic importance of IT for the organization. Factors working against including many risky projects in the portfolio are newness of the IT development staff, a history of development failures, or organizational backwardness in the use of IT (Applegate et al., 2003). A formula for portfolio risk is probably not possible.

This type of risk is not directly addressed by Lucas (1999). His assumption seems to be that management decisions to pursue or not to pursue a project will be based solely on the probability of obtaining return on the individual project. Strategic considerations would enter through probability of successful return for a project type, in this case a strategic project. But there is still no mechanism for considering the group characteristics of a collection of projects.

The second type of risk in the Harvard approach, *project risk,* is very similar to the second probability in Lucas' equation, probability of successful completion of the project. The Harvard approach (Applegate et al., 2003) is indeed assessing the same thing, namely, the likelihood of successful implementation given that the project has been given a green light. However, the output is completely different. Instead of a numerical probability, the Harvard approach yields the result that a project has either high risk, medium risk, or low risk of implementation failure. The risk level is determined by three parameters:

- Size of project for the organization;
- Organizational experience level with the relevant technology; and
- Level of structure of the project.

The matrix in Figure 1 shows how these parameters determine risk level (Applegate et al., 2003).

Larger project size simply intensifies the risk. Thus, if a project is small, has high structure, and the organization is very familiar with the technology, the risk will be very low. If the project is large and the other parameters are the same, the risk becomes merely low. The table entries give small project risk first and then large project risk.

The project structure parameter is interesting. For system developers, programmers, and software engineers, the concept is familiar. It is to what extent the inputs and outputs of the project are specified in advance. A set of financial reports mandated by the government is likely to be very high structure. Inputs, outputs, even formats are likely to be completely specified before project implementation begins. At the other extreme, a project described only as a Web site to improve customer relations has, at the outset, no fixed inputs and outputs and is very low structure.

Probably the best way to test the validity of the matrix is to consider cases. Spectacular failures reveal another aspect of applying the matrix. Consider, for example, the automated baggage handling system at Denver International

Figure 1.

	Low Structure	High Structure
High familiarity with technology	Very low to low risk (easy to mismanage)	Very low to low risk
Low familiarity with technology	High to very high risk	Medium risk

Airport. This project was never completed. In 1992, the Boeing Airport Engineering (BAE) company was awarded a contract to build an automated baggage handling system for the new Denver airport under construction. Although BAE was possibly the most experienced company in the world in baggage handling technology, this project was much larger than any previously attempted anywhere and involved a number of new and untested features. So we conclude large size and low familiarity with the technology. In determining the level of structure of the project, we find it was highly structured to begin with, but BAE was unable to prevent numerous and large change requests from being honored (Applegate, Monteleagre, Nelson, & Knoop, 1996). So, in practice, the project had low structure. The matrix yields the result for large size, low structure, low familiarity as: Very high risk.

I believe one can have more confidence in this type of output than in a numerical probability. But the question still arises, what do I, as a manager, do, when told that a project has high or medium or low implementation risk? The Harvard approach (Applegate et al., 1996) includes management advice tailored to each quadrant of the matrix. For example, high structured-high familiarity projects are very easy to manage but are unfortunately rare. A portfolio with 90% of such projects will not require highly skilled IT staff and will be very safe. Whereas, high structure-low familiarity projects require highly skilled IT people and commonly long delays will occur because technology turns out to be inadequate for the task. Low-structure projects require extensive structured user involvement and formal change-control to prevent runaway. If low-structure projects are also low-familiarity, complete user commitment to design at the beginning is essential, but it may be best to break the project into smaller pieces that use familiar technology (Applegate et al., 2003).

By contrast, Lucas' (1999) answer to the question of what to do with his probability estimates of successful return is this (emphasis as in original):

Anything less than a probability of 1 for a return on the type of investment and a probability of 1 for conversion success dramatically reduces the probability that you will be successful in obtaining a return on an IT investment. (p. 39)

Since virtually every real-life case will have probabilities less than one, it is hard to see how this advice can help management.

The Harvard approach recently supplemented the management advice given above with conflicting advice formulated during the height of the dot.com bubble in 1999 (Applegate et al., 2003; Austin & Nolan, 1999). The felt need for extreme speed in that era resulted in advice to ignore formal planning and, in effect, treat every project as a low-structured project. The management challenges posed by low-structure projects are glossed over. They find that somehow "users are forced" to consider the consequences of change requests and that "a natural discipline evolves to control unreasonable user requests" (Applegate et al., 2003, p.596). Rotsa ruck.

Conclusions about User Value

So where does this leave us? What can a decision-maker do when confronted with the question of the value of a proposed IT project for the organization? We can safely say that if costs and benefits can be quantified in a clear way, then traditional measures such as ROI can be used to determine the value of the project for the organization. The organization should have determined what measures are appropriate for its purposes, whether ROI or some other way of estimating cost/benefit values for the organization.

And for the large class of cases where a project is in some way of strategic importance, then the fit of the project to the overall strategic goals of the organization needs to be assessed. This assessment typically requires management experience, both in general and with this organization. If IT personnel contribute to the assessment, they also must have management as well as technical expertise, and certainly need to be competent to assess the fit of an IT project to the organization's strategic goals.

Finally, for the important assessment of the likelihood of successful completion of a project, both technical and managerial experience are needed, both in general and for the particular organization.

As I stated at the beginning of the chapter, considerations about the value of IT for an organization become ethical considerations through the duties acquired by IT personnel and managers in fulfilling their roles. We have concluded that experience plays an indispensable role in making the value assessments necessary to fulfill professional and managerial duties. There is a place for research findings about IT value to which managers and IT personnel should pay attention. It may be, for example, that a scheme like that proposed by Lucas (1999) could be made less "subjective" and hence more reliable for managerial decision making. There is definitely a place for more research into the causes of project failures, but, at the present time, a manager or an IT professional cannot rely solely on such research untempered by experience. This is an ethical matter: To do so could be a failure to fulfill one's professional or managerial duty through mistaken confidence in imperfect research findings.

References

Applegate, L. M., Austin, R. D., McFarlan, & F. W. (2003). *Corporate information systems: Text and cases* (6th ed.). New York: McGraw-Hill Irwin.

Applegate, L. M., Monteleagre, R., Nelson, H., & Knoop, C.-I. (1996). BAE automated systems: Denver International Airport baggage-handling system. *Harvard Business School Case* 9-396-311. Cambridge, MA: Harvard Business School Press.

Austin, R. D., & Nolan, R. L. (1999). Manage ERP initiatives as new ventures, not IT projects. *Harvard Business School Working Paper 99-024*. Cambridge, MA: Harvard Business School Press.

Black, M. (1967). Probability. In P. Edwards (Ed.), *The encyclopedia of philosophy, vol. 6* (pp. 464-478). New York: Collier-Macmillan.

Brynjolfsson, E. (1992). The productivity paradox of information technology: Review and assessment. *Communications of the ACM, 16*(12), 66-73.

Helm, L. (1999). Productivity jumps with help from Net. *Los Angeles Times,* June 30, Part A, A-1.

King, J., & Konsynski, B. (1990). Singapore TradeNet: A tale of one city. *Harvard Business School Case 9-191-009*. Cambridge, MA: Harvard Business School Press.

Loveman, G. W. (1988). An assessment of the productivity impact of information technologies. *Management in the 1990s*. Cambridge, MA: Sloan School of Management, MIT.

Lucas, Jr., H. C. (1999). *Information technology and the productivity paradox*. New York: Oxford University Press.

Mandel, M. J. (2004). Productivity: Will the miracle last? *BusinessWeek*, July 12, 32-35.

Morrison, C.J., & Berndt, E.R. (1990). *Assessing the productivity of information technology equipment in the U.S. manufacturing industries*. National Bureau of Economic Research Working Paper #3582, January.

Roach, S. (1991). Services under siege: The restructuring imperative. *Harvard Business Review*, Sept.-Oct., 82-92.

Satzinger, J. W., Jackson, R. B., & Burd, S. D. (2004). *Systems analysis and design in a changing world*. Boston, MA: Thomson Course Technology.

Standish Group. (1994). CHAOS. Retrieved on October 21, 2004, from www.pm2go.com/sample_research/chaos_1994_1.asp

Endnotes

[1]   The importance of point of view in the definition of value is discussed in Chapter II, A Background in Ethical Theory, "Theory of Value." An object of value is one that answers to the interests one has in the object from a specific point of view.

[2]   See Chapter II, A Background in Ethical Theory, "Theory of Value."

Chapter XII

The Ultimate Value of Technology

In the previous chapter, we saw how difficult it was to determine the value of information technology, even with a clearly defined point of view from which to assess that value, namely, the interests of the organization utilizing the technology. Over and above the point of view of the organization or even the economy as an aggregate of organizations, there are other perspectives to consider. Is it correct to view technology as another enabling value like health and wealth, an all-purpose means that enables us to achieve any number of our ends?[1] Or should technology rather be viewed as an entirely different way of structuring reality? These questions raise broader issues that need to be considered from much wider points of view: What is the value of information technology for humanity as a whole? And finally, what is the value of information technology for *being* as a whole? In considering these questions, we need also to consider whether the value of information technology is best assessed as a part of technology generally, or whether information technology has its own characteristics relevant for assessing its value. I will examine issues concerning technology as a whole in this chapter, and return to the IT-specific issues in the next chapter.

Beyond considering technology and information technology from the point of view of humanity as a whole, it may be necessary to consider technology and information technology from the point of view of *being* as a whole. One could think of the point of view of *being* as a whole as God's point of view, except that many religious conceptions of God assign many different human attributes to God. And so to determine what is valuable from God's point of view would embroil us in major religious disputes about God's nature. Trying to take the point of view of *being* avoids such disputes. Rather, we are asking, what is the value of technology from the point of view of the unfolding or revealing of whatever is, has been, or will come to be?[2]

Even the point of view of humanity is itself very difficult for many people to embrace. Instead, their highest point of view is that of some limited human group, most typically national or social groups, ethnic groups, or economic groups or organizations. Yet even with these difficulties, it is easier to discuss the value of technology and information technology from the point of view of humanity as a whole than it is to discuss these questions from the point of view of *being*. So we will start with the point of view of humanity.

The Point of View of an Intelligent Species

One value—and it is clearly an enabling value for the species as a whole—is the continuation of the species. A second enabling value for the species as a whole is the development of human capacities, most especially highly developed consciousness of the environment and the ability to make changes on the basis of that consciousness. These abilities are what we think of as intelligence in a life form.[3]

No one could deny that human beings have made, and continue to make, sweeping changes in the environment of earth. The development of powerful tools to master the environment continues apace through science and technology. Technology has been responsible for the conquest of disease, and, for many of us, longer, richer, and more comfortable lives. Science, technology, and information technology have also contributed to the amazing growth of consciousness of the past 500 years or so. Yet are we conscious enough? The non-intelligent aspects of human control of the environment are those that threaten not only species survival but also the existence of the ecosystem.

So one basis for the assessment of the value of technology and information technology for the human species as a whole is the point of view of an intelligent species as just explained. Therefore, the ethical question is, how does taking this wider point of view impact how we should act? And what are the ethical principles to be used in making this determination?

Technology and Consciousness

We are indebted to science for the amazing growth in consciousness of our position in the planet and the universe. It is astonishing to remember that only 400 years ago, in the most advanced of European countries, people such as Galileo were under attack for threatening a more limited traditional consciousness. Until very recently, most human beings were conscious of the universe as a three-storied place, with the living in the middle, the dead in the underground, and the gods and spirits in the heavens. In fact, these views continue to be advocated by many religions and are believed by many people. Yet we know from science that they can be at best figuratively true. It is a measure of the intelligence of most believers in Heaven and Hell and the afterlife that suicide is rarely committed to gain entry to a place that does not exist in physical reality. Yet the old beliefs are very natural and persist in some form even when consciousness has advanced beyond them.[4]

Science has, in the past 150 years or so, also made astonishing contributions to our understanding of ourselves as living beings among living beings. The twin discoveries of evolution and genetics have barely been assimilated, even by science itself. Individual living beings are the expression of complex genetic codes honed over time by interaction with the rest of the environment. Even more recent work in ecology has demonstrated the complexity of that interaction. Yet human leaders often don't consider the possibility that human economic activity has to be constrained by the ecosystem.

The disturbing aspects of human control of the environment are those that threaten the existence of the ecosystem. As human systems increase in size, their scope becomes global. The alarming feature of these systems is that there are no automatic features of the ecosystem that can bring things back into balance. As Miriam MacGillis once put it, "we have taken the planet off automatic pilot".[5] We are probably the first species on this planet with the capability of destroying the entire ecosystem, not just in one but a multitude of ways:

- Einstein and Teilhard de Chardin (1964) were impressed with the fact that nuclear weapons gave humankind the capability of extinguishing all life. That we haven't used these weapons in war after their first use is a sign of our intelligence. The fact that these weapons are still around and proliferating is not.

- A "safe" synthetic compound, chlorofluorocarbon, developed in the 1940s for use in air conditioners and aerosol cans turned out to be inert except in the upper atmosphere, where it continues to destroy the ozone layer that protects us from ultraviolet radiation. There are two disturbing implications: (1) There does not seem to be any way that this result of normal chemical engineering could have been predicted. (2) All life has evolved under the protection of the ozone layer; this sudden change has unpredictable consequences for all life forms in the ecosystem. (Asimov & Pohl, 1991).

- The same unpredictable consequences are the result of the addition of gases that are the by-product of industrial technology—called the "greenhouse" gases because they increase the ability of the earth's atmosphere to retain heat, just like the panes of glass in a greenhouse. The most important gas is carbon dioxide, with much of it coming from the burning of fossil fuels in internal combustion engines. The effects produced by the increased carbon dioxide are difficult to predict, but the size of the increase would normally happen over tens of thousands of years. One current predicted consequence, other than warming, is storms of increasing severity. Severe strains on plants and animals are also to be expected (McKibben, 1989, pp. 3-46).

This issue, because it directly affects human economics, has aroused contrary argumentation based on the premise that human economic activity cannot possibly affect the entire environment. This is probably wishful thinking. Science tells us that our atmosphere's composition is not a given; the amount of carbon actually in the atmosphere is about the same as that present in the totality of living beings (the "biomass"). Consequently, adding the carbon locked up in fossils in large quantities is very likely to have an impact.

- Other components of the atmosphere necessary for animal life are also threatened. Oxygen, a highly reactive element, is present in our current atmosphere solely because plants are currently producing it. Almost all current life is oxygen-dependent, and has depended on a constant percentage of about 21% for hundreds of millions of years. A percentage of 25 would cause all organic materials to ignite. With 15%, many forms of oxidation (such as fire) would not occur. (McKibben, 1989, p.157). Thus, the destruction of tropical rain forests, which produce 40% of the world's oxygen, could be a serious threat to the survival of almost all life, including us. We can already see that it cannot be intelligent to treat everything on the planet not already humanized as "natural resources" to be utilized however we please for arbitrary human purposes.

Human beings have, for millennia, treated other species as items to be exploited. While many of the problems just mentioned arose recently as the result of civilization and modern technology, there is evidence that humans were causing extinctions as long as 60,000 years ago. Richard Leakey produces strong evidence that megafauna extinctions in Australia and the Americas were caused in large part by human "overkill" (Leakey & Lewin, 1995, p. 194). These extinctions were selective. The less frequent five previous mass extinctions were caused by environmental catastrophes, very likely asteroid collisions. Human beings are currently causing the sixth mass extinction, all on their own. As much as 50% of all species may be extinct in 100 years (Leakey & Lewin, 1995). Discussions of the negative effects of these extinctions often revolve around the loss of these species for human purposes such as drugs. Once again, "man is the measure of all things," as if it were possible for humankind to exist without other species.

- One of the most mentioned positive factors of human control over the environment through technology, one clear demonstration of our intelligence as a species, has been our ability to conquer disease and extend the human life span. Yet again, we almost always think in terms only of the aims of individual human beings, when sometimes the survival of the species needs to have ethical priority.

Although it is wonderful when humans with life-threatening defects are given normal lives with the aid of technology, from the point of view of the species, it makes no sense for them to reproduce those defects. It should be a matter of personal ethical responsibility not to reproduce genetic defects known to require extensive intervention to have a normal life. As it is, the occurrence of diabetes is increasing rapidly because medical science can treat diabetics well enough to allow diabetics to live long enough to reproduce and produce—diabetic children.

Unlike the Nazis, I am not calling for eugenics or the social elimination of "undesirables," but rather for the awareness of individuals of their ethical responsibility to the species. Because the survival of individuals is not just a matter of their short-term success in the environment, but also how they contribute to the long-term survival of the species, traits advantageous for short-term survival may be disastrous for long-terms species survival.

Eugenics, focusing only on individual short-term goals, is therefore also not the way to fulfill an ethical responsibility to the species. For example, breeding excellent football players could easily have unintended side effects in interacting with the environment.[6]

- The same point applies to genetic manipulation in general. Since genetics are a separate dimension from regular life, there may be unforeseen consequences that do not play out within individual life spans. But if so, then how can "genetic engineering" be safe? We cannot predict the long-range effects of such genetic manipulation as producing a more frost-resistant strawberry. In nature, genetic changes are honed over time against the existing environment. By making changes out of context, we are asking for a disaster as extensive as the disappearance of the ozone layer.

Current uses of genetic engineering show that science itself is not fully conscious of its own relation to the ecosystem. We already have cases in which genetically altered individuals cannot be safely released into the environment. Salmon engineered for increased size are also sterile. Wild female salmon prefer to mate with the larger engineered salmon and thus will produce no offspring. If engineered salmon are introduced into the wild, salmon extinction would be highly probable. Genetically engineered changes are thus being judged only in the context of current benefit to current human aims.

The examples given above strongly suggest that the human propensity to manipulate the environment may very well not be compatible with long-term species survival. Yet what do these examples really show about the value of technology? Is it technology that is at fault or is it the application of technology through human political, social, and economic institutions? This question will be discussed shortly when we consider priorities between competing ethical principles in this area.

Three Relevant Ethical Principles

These examples suggest two conclusions about the point of view of human beings as a species:

- First, human beings acting independently in their own interests will not necessarily act in the best interest of the species;
- Second, the ecosystem of which we are a part cannot be treated as an external entity to be exploited for arbitrary human purposes.

Therefore, from an ethical point of view, there are two corresponding directives:

- **Species Survival Principle:** Principles of action governing the use of technology must grant considerations of the survival of the species higher priority than any individual or group interests.
- **Ecosystem Principle:** Principles furthering the continuation of the human species must consider the survival of the ecosystem of which human beings are a part as a higher priority.

Members of a species acting from their consciousness of their place in the ecosystem would probably not manipulate of the environment anywhere near the amount we consider routine for our own purposes. Dolphins and whales may be examples of beings following such principles. It has been pointed out that these cetaceans have brains at least as complex as ours. An individual of any species must expend enormous resources to maintain brains of great complexity—in the case of human beings, fully 40% of our energy budget is spent on our brains. If these organs were not of use to the individual, evolution would rapidly select them away. Yet dolphins and whales do not use their complex brains to manipulate the environment. The conclusion is that, although the complexity of their brains must be of great use to the cetaceans, we do not have a clue as to what these uses might be. They are definitely not using them to manipulate their environment (Kaiser, 1990).

Similar observations apply to extraterrestrials. It currently appears that planetary systems are quite common, and that planetary systems will very often develop in similar ways to our own solar system, with several earth-sized rocky inner planets and several gas giants. So there are likely many water planets in the universe with similar physical characteristics as Earth.

We are looking for radio signals from beings with similar tendencies as ours to expand heedlessly into their environment. If my observations here are on the right track, beings interested in sending such signals may very well have a short window of existence in the life of a planet. In fact, until we gain greater insight into what we are doing as a species, thoughtless expansion of human life or terrestrial life into the cosmos may be, from the point of view of everything else (the point of view of *being*), more like a disease spreading than progress. Human beings may be, at this point, like a disease in the ecosystem, especially if the concept of disease is correctly understood: A disease is a misunderstanding between two species. Our misunderstanding may be that we can exist completely apart from our biological basis in the ecosystem.

Technology, in many ways, reflects this separation from the ecosystem. Very often, the intelligence of the human species is thought of only in terms of our ability to manipulate the environment, and the more manipulation, the greater the intelligence. Indeed, many scientists and technologists hold what might be called a "manifest destiny" view of technology—that it is our goal or even duty to change the environment as much as possible, and to spread ourselves as widely as possible.[7] We will call this the Technology Principle: Technological progress is inevitable, unstoppable, and mostly beneficial. The results of technology come about through its unimpeded progress. Hence, technological development must have priority over other considerations.

It is fairly obvious that the Technology Principle, the Ecosystem Principle, and the Species Survivial Principle are not compatible. If human survival and survival of the ecosystem have priority, then technological progress does not have priority. The reason for the open-endedness of the Technology Principle is that it is not uncommon for technology developed for one use to find another, essential, use later on. For this reason, proponents of the Technology Principle point out that you can never have too much technological development. Also, unimpeded growth in technological research and development is thought to be essential in correcting technology's flaws. For these reasons, it can be argued that actually the Technology Principle is the best way of serving human survival and survival of the ecosystem. We will return to this discussion shortly, after a closer examination of technology itself.

The Nature of Technology

I will consider technology in three stages:

1. The traditional technology of agriculture and cities that enabled the rise of civilization, roughly 10,000 years old;
2. Modern technology enabled by science, about 500 years old; and
3. Information technology, about 50-60 years old.

The use of any technology enabling more than hunter-gatherer societies takes up a remarkably short portion of human existence on the planet. Using current estimates of the presence of human beings of our species for the last 250,000 years, civilization has been a possible human mode of existence for 10,000 years, no more than 4% of humanity's time on earth. Joseph Tainter (1988) argues in his book, *The Collapse of Complex Societies,* that, so far, civilizations other than our current one have been unable to avoid collapsing under their own weight. He thinks our current civilization is different from previous ones in having modern technology to increase resources and thus at least postpone collapse. [8]

Indeed, it is because of technology—at least technology in the service of increasing our consciousness of our place on the planet—that we can even begin to have any hope of overcoming the difficulties in our current position. For it is largely science and the technological apparatus necessary for science that is responsible for all the knowledge underpinning our discussion so far. If our intelligence has failed us in leading us in the direction of destroying our own ecosystem, it has not failed us in revealing this very situation to us.

Yet neither science nor technology contains within itself directions out of the current situation. Indeed, defenders of the Technology Principle tend to argue that for any problem, there is a further technological fix. There are two real problems with this view: First, there is no good reason to believe it; and second, the fixes take us farther and farther away from any recognizably sustainable world. Not only do we end up existing for the sake of our technology, but the technological apparatus becomes increasingly susceptible to catastrophic failure, as Asimov pointed out in his science-fiction novel *The Caves of Steel* (1954).[9] Modern technology takes us in directions not previously encountered in our environment. Our changes tend to have "side effects," unpredictable and dangerous consequences. Chlorofluorocarbons and their effect on the ozone layer ought to be more than sufficient to put us on notice that we really do not know what we're doing with our technological changes. Further technological fixes to the ozone layer may very well have quite different unintended consequences on the rest of the ecosystem. There is simply no way of ruling out such a possibility.

Some authors actually embrace the possibility of leaving the current basis of life completely behind. Perhaps the most extreme version of the Technology Principle is that of the roboticist Hans Moravec. Moravec (1988) suggests that it is time to leave DNA-based life behind in favor of the superior creations of the human mind. These "Mind Children" (the title of his book) will become our progeny through a process of "downloading."

To think that such a process is even possible requires belief in a metaphysical view of human beings that is an unofficial part of the methodology of modern science. This view is that human beings are radically different from other animals in having nonphysical minds as well as physical bodies. Unfortunately, no account of how a relation between a physical and a nonphysical thing is possible has ever made much sense. The first clear statement of the mind-body dichotomy by Descartes in 1641 states and fails to deal with the same difficulties about their relation that persist to this day. Moravec (1988), as a good scientific materialist, merely makes the mind physical. We can "download" patterns of information, and if that was all there were to human consciousness and intelligence, a (very) large collection of leather-bound volumes would be interchangeable with any human being.

The Point of View of
Modern Technology

It is very important to recognize fully how deep these problems with technology are. Technologists tend to be very intelligent people. It may seem obvious to me that manipulation of genetic material is extremely dangerous given the nature of how species relate to the environment, but bioengineers are similarly baffled by objections to their seemingly totally beneficial attempts to provide more food for people who are malnourished. It was the philosopher Martin Heidegger who saw most clearly that *modern technology has its own point of view* that is completely separate from any other structure of human aims and purposes. The critical feature of modern technology is its willingness to treat anything as a resource to be reordered in the furtherance of human aims. Heidegger, in his essay *The Question Concerning Technology* (1955), concludes that modern technology is an independent force in human existence. It builds a new and incompatible order on top of what was there, primarily in order to extract and store energy for later uses. The point of view of modern technology regards everything as a potential resource, as "standing reserve" to be used or reused later in other processes of the same kind. A forest has status only as a timber resource. Land itself is only a resource for the building industry. Even human beings themselves, from this point of view, become "human resources." Or they become "consumers." Or ill people become a "supply of patients for a clinic." Many distinctive modern technologies embody this notion of "standing reserve" in their very conception. Thus, electric power, whether in the form of available current or batteries, is always entirely standing reserve, on hand for potential use.

This way of looking at things, insofar as it ignores the previous pattern of processes, uses, and ends, is inherently "violent" in its effects on those processes. It is also a critical part of the point of view of modern technology that technology continues to present itself to us as a mere means, an enabler for our ends. But it is impossible to "place" technology ethically in a correct way without the realization that *modern technology has its own ends,* which are to reorder everything as standing reserve in yet-undisclosed ways. As Julian Young (2002) puts it in his admirable and lucid study of Heidegger on these issues:

...human beings [become] the most important [raw material] because as well as being available for manipulation and exploitation as productive units they are also the manipulators and exploiters, as it were the portals through which the global system of production and consumption—a system which, to repeat, is circular and so pointless—maintains itself. (p. 46)[10]

Here, then, is the ethical point. The general principle for the determination of the priority of ethical principles has all along been that higher order principles settle disputes between lower level principles that cannot be settled on their own. The principle to serve technological ends cannot have priority over all other principles—the reason that technology's own ends would be furthered is not sufficient to establish this priority. There are indeed conflicting alternative principles to the Technology Principle, namely, the Species Survival Principle and the Ecosystem Principle, which have been advocated by many in the past 30 to 40 years. So our procedure will be, first, to examine the nature of these conflicting principles, and then to see why the basis for a higher order principle has to be as general as that provided by Heidegger's (1927, 1955) analysis of ways of bringing things into being.

Technology vs. the Environment

The negative effects of human beings on their environment have been discussed by a number of different thinkers from a variety of perspectives. By no means do all feel that the threat to the environment and to human survival is due to technology. In fact, some feel that technology is the solution. The following table (Table 1) captures, I believe, many of the major viable possible positions on the ecological crisis and possible solutions to the problem that have surfaced in the past 20 to 30 years. After considering the merits of these positions and solutions, I believe we will be in a position to decide on a viable ethical principle concerning technology and the environment.

The possible solutions in the table fall into the following main types: (1) Work within the current economic and technological systems, but be more careful (Gore, 1992; Winner, 1977); (2) Change the current economic and social structure and use technology to solve environmental problems (Commoner,

Table 1. Proposed solutions to the ecological crisis

Author	Critical ecosystem stress	Primary cause	Primary solution
Ehrlich (1968; 2000, 322)	Overpopulation	Wasteful consumption by rich, increased numbers of others	Sustainable society & technology
Commoner (1971, 191)	Post-WWII ecologically insensitive technologies	Profits before ecological consequences	Transform production to take ecology into account
Schumacher (1973,293-297)	Economic growth	Inefficiencies in large-scale institutions	Downsize units of production; adopt human scale for technology
Winner (1977, 19-30)	Careless application of technology	Lack of awareness of consequences of technology	Technology with much more stringent controls
Fuller (1981 xvii-xxix, xxxvi-xxxviii)	Energy crisis	Social and political institutions	Change application of technology to improving global standard of living
McKibben (1989, 166-170, 213-217)	Atmosphere destruction	Human hegemony over nature	Adopt attitude that rest of creation matters for its own sake
Foreman (1991, 25-36)	Excessive human development, hegemony	Principle of humans first	Return much developed land to wilderness
Gore 1992, 295-369)	Dysfunctional overconsumption	Addiction to consumption	Social and economic policies--within current framework–for sustainability

1971; Ehrlich, 1998, 2000; Fuller, 1981); (3) Change the current economic, social, and spiritual structure to reduce or eliminate dependence on technology (Schumacher, 1973); (4) Change current ethical and social structures to remove human beings from a position of primacy (Foreman, 1991; McKibben, 1989).

It is interesting that none of these authors sees the problem to be technology itself. Technology is, for most, an enabling neutral means that can be employed for any problem, including problems with the environment. Yet it is already abundantly clear that none of their solutions based on this premise can work. This can be made clearer by considering the ethical status of each type of problem and solution:

1.   Working within the current socioeconomic technological structure, as recommended by social theorist Langdon Winner and near-President Al Gore. For Winner (1977), the relevant ethical noncompliance category is *mistake*.[11] We simply had no idea technology could have such consequences, and we will be "more careful" in the future. The example of chlorofluorocarbons, not available in 1977 when Winner was writing, shows the bankruptcy of this approach. There is simply no way we could

have been more careful. For Gore (1992), on the other hand, the relevant noncompliance category is *shortcoming*. [12] We know that unsustainable consumption is destroying the planet, but we just have to be firm about not consuming so much and achieving sustainability; and we should alter our social and economic situations accordingly. Although this will clearly help and some individuals will be motivated to reduce consumption, it does not handle cases where the results are more indirect, such as global warming. A society can be efficient in the sense of not consuming wastefully and still be very destructive to the environment. Gore's message that we just need to get the economy back on track in working to avoid wasteful consumption does not address many aspects of the problem.

2.   Ehrlich, Commoner, and Fuller all see the problem as residing in the social and economic structure. The noncompliance category is *mistake,* and the mistake is an inappropriate social and economic structure that needs to be changed to get the world back on track. Ehrlich (1968, 2000) originally blamed overpopulation, and still thinks it an important factor to be solved by appropriate social and political structures. Commoner (1971) and Fuller (1981) both believe, instead, that there would be plenty to go around if social and economic production facilities were properly organized. So for them, overpopulation is not a major consideration. Commoner emphasizes the contrast between the older, pre-World-War II technologies and the newer technologies adopted since then: Pasturing animals vs. factory farming; maintaining soil fertility through crop rotation vs. chemical fertilizers; biodegradable soap vs. detergents; natural vs. synthetic textiles. Production technologies with intense impact on the environment have displaced those that did not. These new technologies are more profitable for the producers—the farmers, cleaning product manufacturers, and textile producers. Commoner's solution is to reverse this kind of thinking at the level of social institutions. But the point is that the technologist simply may not care that much, or even if he does, the solution may be (as happened in 1965) to produce biodegradable detergent molecules with benzene components making them even more toxic to the environment (Commoner, 1971,). Commoner is on the right track, but the question is, what in technology leads in these directions? The answer has to be technology's tendency to have its own ends and its goal of remaking the entire world by utilizing it as resources for its own applications. Similar replacements took place during the Industrial Revolution—old ways of doing things were replaced with newer, faster, less

environmentally friendly ways. Consider the mechanization of weaving looms that gave rise to the Luddites and to the "dark, Satanic mills" described by Blake (1804).

Fuller (1981) looks to technology as the solution to current social problems of poverty and inequality. For Fuller, it is simple wrongheadedness in the application of technology that is producing a crisis. If technology could be completely subordinated to appropriate social and economic ends, there would be no problem. Fuller's hopes seem beside the point given the ecological problems raised by technology. Also, what institutions are going to ensure that technology gets used in these beneficial social ways? Fuller seems to think that the technologists themselves are capable of this, but this would require them to have authority over social and economic institutions, which they hardly seem qualified to exercise.

3. Schumacher (1973) sees technology and social structures moving in tandem to produce the problem. Both require things to be done on a larger scale than necessary, and produce detrimental results. For Schumacher, the solution is simply to scale down expectations, both social and economic as well as technological. There is some overlap with other solutions: Small applications are more likely to be sustainable, and are less likely to contain inefficiencies destructive of the ecosystem. Indeed, his "small" applications look very much like instances of technology that are not modern, in Heidegger's (1955) terms. For Schumacher, what matters is smallness as a spiritual correlate to technology appropriate to human needs and to the environment. Ultimately, Schumacher is calling for a change of heart to a more human scale as the basis for the relevant downsizing to sustainability. But his solution, like Fuller's (1981), does not deal directly with ecological problems. He does indicate that smaller scale, more responsive systems are less likely to cause environmental damage, but these consequences seem to be desirable by-products of smallness. And so his solution leaves the ecological problem unsolved.

4. The final group of views requiring a radical change of heart in one's relation to the earth would, unlike the solutions just discussed, be *sufficient* to solve the problem. But they suffer from defects similar to using *feelings* as a basis for ethics.[13] Basing any obligation to the species or the ecosystem on how you feel about it, makes it seem more like a special interest or hobby than a genuinely ethical matter.[14] Second, as we saw in considering the Principles of Justice (Rawls, 1999) and of relations between peoples, it is important that ethics require only that the basis of

social cooperation be shared. Ethics cannot and should not require the adoption of deep-seated comprehensive views about the nature of reality because they cannot realistically be shared as the basis of social cooperation.[15] Foreman's (1991) and McKibben's (1989) views about putting human beings in a less exalted place would, if adopted, solve the problem, but would require something close to a religious or spiritual conversion on the part of everyone in the society.

Heidegger's (1955) analysis of technology can provide a basis for workable ethical principles, even though it also can seem "religious" or "spiritual." But rather than calling for specific changes in social or economic or technological systems—or even in feelings—we acknowledge the priority of bringing things into being over the specifically technological way of bringing things into being. To do this is to take the point of view of Being. We then have a basis for considering the priorities between the Technology Principle, the Species Survival Principle, and the Ecosystem Principle.

We have an example of what it would be like to give the Technology Principle priority over the Species Survival Principle—it is Hans Moravec's (1988) proposal to leave DNA behind in favor of the creations of the human mind. Unfortunately, if his metaphysical view of mind is incorrect, there will only be machines performing meaningless operations. I believe the correct current view of the mind/body situation is that of the physicist Roger Penrose (1989), who argues that scientific methodology as presently conceived is incomplete and in its current form unable to deal with the mind/body problem. As we noted before, there has been no good explanation of how a nonphysical mind and a physical body interact since 1641 when Descartes first formulated these views.

Science also has a "hidden" place for human beings that can't be eradicated. Science views objects as what Heidegger (1927) calls "present-at-hand." Objects considered in this way lack functional and value characteristics, the very characteristics most important in the environments of living beings for species survival. On the other hand, objects viewed as "ready-to-hand" are viewed in terms of their manipulation and use by human beings in a typical human environmental context, that is, where one is a physical body among other physical bodies. But even the most theoretical physics does not and cannot completely abstract from a human presence—both quantum physics and relativity theory require an *observer,* a point of consciousness that reflects its environment. Tucked into every representation of the world, whether scientific or everyday, is a conscious point of view.

So, if we are choosing priorities between the Species Survival Principle and the Technology Principle from the point of view of Being, at this point, the Species Survival Principle must have priority: If technology is able to bring things into being, it is only through the agency of human beings that, at this point, requires the species in order to survive.

There are two other possible priorities to consider: (1) the priority between the Technology Principle and the Ecosystem Principle; and (2) the priority between the Species Survival Principle and the Ecosystem Principle.

If the Technology Principle is allowed a higher priority than the Ecosystem Principle, the aims of the ecosystem will be served only if they promote technological aims. Which principle gets higher priority depends on high-level beliefs about human technology and its relation to nature. If one believes that technology can correct its own errors in a timely manner and that a policy of unregulated technological progress is otherwise most conducive to overall human progress, then technological progress becomes the ultimate value and touchstone for policy. If one believes human technology has built-in unanticipated conflicts with the ecosystem, then a policy of minimum mutilation of the ecosystem is called for. An important point here is that the principles governing the overall utilization of technology, because of the far-reaching nature of that utilization, have to be higher level even than Principles of Justice (Rawls, 1999) and even those of principles of international justice.[16]

Could the Species Survival Principle have priority over the Ecosystem Principle? Since species survival depends on survival of the ecosystem, such a priority would not seem to make sense. One set of circumstances where it might make sense is if we covertly have in mind eliminating the ecosystem in favor of some substitute supplied by technology. But to believe that species survival would be best served that way would require the priority of the Technology Principle over the Ecosystem Principle. And in the previous paragraph, I supplied reasons for rejecting that priority.

Another possible case where the Species Survival Principle might have priority over the Ecosystem Principle is if it turned out that the only way that the human species could survive would be by destroying or seriously damaging the ecosystem. It may well be that the kinds of changes necessary for the human species to be compatible with the ecosystem are simply not practicable. Different priorities would then result in two somewhat different doomsday scenarios: (1) Either human beings diminish in numbers, restrict their manipulation of the environment even when that might yield short-term benefits for the species, but allow the rest of the ecosystem to take its course; or (2) We prolong species survival as long as possible even if it would result in the extermination of all other species on the planet. These are both really scenarios for species suicide, slow or quick. The first scenario acknowledges priority of the Ecosystem Principle.

The second doomsday scenario, in which we eliminate all other life on the planet in order to preserve the life of our own species, is the only one where the Species Survival Principle has priority over the Ecosystem Principle. It is almost certainly a fantasy that we could survive in the absence of any other life, and such a fantasy would probably include the presumption that technology can replace the extensive life support we depend on. So it comes down to whether, in going extinct as a species, we take all other life with us. After all, we would no longer need the ecosystem as support, so the grounds for the priority of the Ecosystem Principle would no longer apply. For this final case, we need to appeal to another point of view, that of Being itself.

Otherwise, there seem to be good reasons for the priority of the Ecosystem Principle over the Species Survival Principle, and the priority of both over the Technology Principle.

The Point of View of *Being* Itself

The point of view of the human species, even as an intelligent species, still considers us as a part of the ecosystem. Over and above that, we are part of the ebb and flow of *being* itself, of the coming to presence and passing away of all things. Heidegger (1955) does not believe that humanity can be the master of *being*, and thus the introduction by humanity of any new mode of being such as technology is quite dangerous. Over and above any danger to the ecosystem, there is a danger of disrupting *being* itself, for there is more to *being* than the ecosystem. The ecosystem depends on the rest of what there is for its substratum; plants synthesize food from the elements and sunlight. There are levels of organization in the weather and the seasons other than those contained in animals and plants that are necessary for their existence. To say that these levels of organization are mere physical processes is exactly the point of view of modern technology. The same would apply to human intelligence itself. Another way of looking at it: If intelligence in the universe appeared only in the form of human beings, then it probably does not appear anywhere at all.

I believe the same considerations of minimum mutilation of the ecosystem may apply as well to *being* itself. If we can accept that there may be more to *being* than even living beings and that, as a species, we have a duty to respect *being*, then we have reason to behave ethically, even in these most extreme circumstances a species has to face. Thus, the ultimate ethical principle may be to demonstrate the awareness of our species of our place within *being* as we leave it, and not have our final message be a path of destruction through the rest of what is.[17] The anthropologist Claude Levi-Strauss (1968) put it this way:

...no species, not even our own, can take the fact of having been on earth for one or two million years—since, in any case, man's stay here will one day come to an end—as an excuse for appropriating the world as if it were a thing and behaving on it with neither decency nor discretion. (p. 508)

References

Asimov, I. (1954). *The caves of steel.* New York: HarperCollins.

Asimov, I., & Pohl, F. (1991). *Our angry earth.* New York: Tom Dougherty Associates.

Bloke, W. (1804). The new Jerusalem. Retrieved on August 10, 2005, from http://eserver.org/poetry/

Commoner, B. (1971). *The closing circle.* New York: Knopf.

Crick, F. (1981). *Life itself.* New York: Simon and Schuster.

Dawkins, R. (1976). *The selfish gene.* New York: Oxford University Press.

Descartes, R. (1641). *Meditations.* Retrieved on June 7, 2004, from www.classicallibrary.org/descartes/meditations/

Diamond, J. (2005). *Collapse: How societies choose to fail or succeed. New York:* Viking Books.

Ehrlich, P. (1968). *The population bomb.* New York: Ballantine Books.

Ehrlich, P. (2000). *Human natures.* New York: Penguin Group.

Foreman, D. (1991). *Confessions of an eco-warrior*. New York: Harmony Books.

Fuller, B. (1981). *Critical path*. New York: St. Martin's Press.

Gore, A. (1992). *Earth in the balance*. New York: Houghton Mifflin.

Heidegger, M. (1927). *Sein und zeit* (translated as *Being and time*). New York: Harper & Row.

Heidegger, M. (1955). The question concerning technology. In *The question concerning technology and other essays*, pp. 3-36. New York: Harper & Row.

Kaiser, D. (1990). Dolphin consciousness. Retrieved on June 7, 2004, from http://home.onemain.com/~dk1008206/html/dolph1.htm

Leakey, R., & Lewin, R. (1995). *The sixth extinction*. New York: Doubleday.

Levi-Strauss, C. (1968). *The origin of table manners*. New York: Harper & Row.

McKibben, B. (1989). *The end of nature*. New York: Doubleday.

Moravec, H. (1988). *Mind children*. Cambridge, MA: Harvard University Press.

Penrose, R. (1989). *The emperor's new mind*. Oxford, UK: Oxford University Press.

Rawls, J. (1999). *A theory of justice* (rev.ed.). Cambridge, MA: Harvard University Press.

Schultz, R. A. (2000). Intelligent life on earth: The pros and cons. Presented at *the 2000 Conference of the International Association for the Management of Technology*, Miami, FL, January 29-23.

Schumacher, E. F. (1973). *Small is beautiful*. New York: Harper & Row.

Tainter, J. (1988). *The collapse of complex societies*. Cambridge, UK: Cambridge University Press.

Teilhard de Chardin, P. (1964). *The future of man*. New York: Harper & Row.

Wachowski, A., & Wachowski, L. (1999). *The matrix* [Film]. Burbank, CA: Warner Bros.

Winner, L. (1977). *Autonomous technology*. Cambridge, MA: MIT Press.

Young, J. (2002). *Heidegger's later philosophy*. Cambridge, UK: Cambridge University Press.

Endnotes

1   An enabling value is a value that allows an individual or group to pursue its more particular goals. Health and wealth are the best examples for individuals. See Chapter II, A Background in Ethical Theory "Theory of Value."

2   Martin Heidegger (1927) was the philosopher who developed this notion of *being*.

3   The next several pages contain material from my paper, "Intelligent Life on Earth, the Pros and Cons," presented at the 2000 Conference of the International Association for the Management of Technology, Miami, FL. Through technical error, this material does not appear in the proceedings of the conference.

4   The Heavens Gate group in San Diego to some extent combined both world views by committing mass suicide to join aliens supposedly circling the earth in spaceships. Thus, they combined a nonphysical transition from life to "another plane" with a physical location to which their disembodied spirits would be moving.

5   The quote is from a talk given to Beyond War in November 1986. For current information about Sr. MacGillis, see www.genesisfarm.org

6   The proper understanding of the relation between genes and their expression in individuals is critical for the ethics of species survival, but very difficult. For a clear understanding of the genetic side (but not the ethics) see Dawkins (1976).

7   For example, Francis Crick (1981, 117-129) has even suggested "seeding" terrestrial life on other planets.

8   Jared Diamond in his book Collapse (2005) is not as positive about the ability of technology to prevent collapse.

9   Asimov's novel, like many good science fiction novels, reveals hidden consequences of current unquestioned assumptions by pushing them toward their limits. In the novel, set several thousand years in the future, some human beings have colonized planets in other star systems. However, further colonization from earth is prevented by the evolution of a disease-free environment on the other planets. Meanwhile, earth itself has evolved into totally enclosed mega-cities with totally engineered environments with a population of 8 billion and climbing. The environment on

earth extrapolated in the novel is present-day New York City, and the criticism made of the environment is a cogent one, namely, that the complexity required to sustain such an artificial and complex environment is fragile and that unexpected disruptions are likely to be catastrophic. The solution, however, is merely another version of Crick's (1981): Export people to areas in which there is more space. One must wonder why a species so clearly unable to live within the parameters of its environment will do better when given more space

[10] The most chilling image of the film *The Matrix* (Wachowski & Wachowski, 1999) is of banks of human beings become pure standing reserve.

[11] Recall from Chapter III, The Context of IT Ethical Issues, "Partial Compliance," that the three noncompliance categories are mistake, shortcoming, and evil.

[12] Recall from Chapter III, The Context of IT Ethical Issues, "Partial Compliance," that the three noncompliance categories are mistake, shortcoming, and evil.

[13] See Chapter II, A Background in Ethical Theory, "Theories of Right: Intuitionist vs. End-Based vs. Duty-Based."

[14] Personal or organizational recycling or Earth Day activities like cleaning beaches are praiseworthy activities. The only danger is to think that if we recycle and pick up after ourselves, the major ecological problem will be thereby solved.

[15] See Chapter II, A Background in Ethical Theory, "Theory of Justice."

[16] And, therefore, such principles also need to be constraints on the behavior of multinational corporations.

[17] In the next chapter, I develop some additional considerations.

Chapter XIII

The Ultimate Value of Information Technology

In order to conclude our discussion of the value of information technology, we need to answer these questions: What characteristics does IT share with modern technology generally? What is its place with respect to the rest of technology and with respect to the rest of the world? The goal of this chapter is to formulate how information technology might interact with ethical principles required at the species level, ecosystem level, and the level of *being* as a whole. I also want to consider the impact of these ethical principles on our responsibilities as IT professionals.

The most positive feature of information technology is its potential to contribute to the increase in human consciousness by making more knowledge more widely available. Yet it can just as easily enable questionable applications of technology that further our extinction as a species or the destruction of the ecosystem. Let us begin by asking of information technology the questions we asked about technology generally: Is information technology a neutral means? Does it have its own ends and point of view?

Modern Technology and IT

We saw in the previous chapter that modern technology is *not* neutral; its use initiates a sequence of changes that takes it to consequences beyond human calculation (Heidegger, 1955). Modern technology has its own point of view and its own ends, primarily to build a new and incompatible order on top of what was there before, in order to extract and store energy for later uses. Although modern technology is an independent force in human existence, it continues to present itself to us as a mere means, an enabler for our other ends. Its way of looking at things, insofar as it ignores the previous pattern of processes, uses, and ends, is inherently "violent" in its effects on those processes. It is always concerned with obtaining the maximum yield for minimum expense (Heidegger, 1955; Young, 2002).

Information technology, not surprisingly, has affinities to and differences from modern technology. IT, like modern technology, is very definitely not a neutral enabling means; it contains its own point of view and specific ends. Yet unlike modern technology, IT does not have the aim of replacing the existing world with its own reality. Rather, it constructs a parallel digital reality with its own relation to our world.

There may occasionally be an IT application that is a mere means, but the functional characteristics that make IT so valuable do not operate in this restricted way. Those characteristics, discussed in Chapter I, are speed of information processing, size of information storage capacity, availability of information at any location, and easy reproduction of information. In order to exploit these characteristics, IT applications need to be part of IT *systems*, with a minimum scope of an organizational department. Usually they work better with a scope of the organization as a whole, and potentially with global scope for organizations that interact through the Internet with customers, suppliers, or other stakeholders. Since 1990, Enterprise Resource Planning (ERP), functionally integrated software, has become popular. Data entered anywhere in the organization is available throughout the organization, everywhere and immediately. Benefits include savings on operations, responsiveness, improved sales, and less frustration (Brady, Monk, & Wagner, 2001).

ERP illustrates a growing tendency of IT to develop its own ends and point of view. In older, traditional systems, the aim of an IT implementation is to capture the logic of the business processes it is automating, but with ERP, everyone initially agrees that an integrated system may require drastic changes to preexisting business processes. The older ideal of faithfully reflecting business processes in an automated system has been superseded. Now the aims of the systems (especially integration) take priority (Brady, Monk, & Wagner, 2001).

But let us first look more closely at the original idea of automation, of translating business processes done manually into automated business processes. The idea is to replace processing of information done by hand, by human minds with the aid of paper, with information processing done by computer. So the aims of information technology are initially narrower than those of modern technology. The aim is not to *replace* the original information-providers with an entirely new structure, but rather to speed up and otherwise make more efficient selected components of the process of gathering, storing, and manipulating information.[1] Within the system, information is reduced to some binary representation (ASCII or Unicode for written text, various formats such as JPEG and GIF for pictorial representation, and various custom schemes for "unusual" information).

As we saw in Chapter XI, Valuing Information Technology, this process can have value for the organization that does it—operations are faster and more accurate. As we also saw, there are some intervening variables that can prevent an organization from realizing these values. When we begin looking at IT for similarities and differences from modern technology as a whole, the interesting and disturbing question is whether IT development is or would be persisted in *even if IT did not add value to the organization.* The suspicion would then be that the special point of view and ends of modern technology were driving its development.

As we also saw in Chapter XI, there are situations in which, although value may not be added, organizational survival may require implementing IT anyway. Clear examples include: matching the IT of competitors, and avoiding loss of control of the business.

In the case of IT, do we see those distinctive marks of modern technology's intent to impose itself on the world and to replace the existing order of information with its own constructs? If we do see this, it is as a marketing plan for Microsoft (and other large IT firms) rather than an inherent feature of information technology itself. In fact, the current debate over Nicholas Carr's contention that IT has lost its strategic importance can be seen as a debate over whether the (general) Technology Principle applies to IT (Carr, 2003, 2004). The Technology Principle (as discussed in Chapter XII) was: Technological progress is inevitable, unstoppable, and mostly beneficial. The results of technology come about through its unimpeded progress. Hence, technological development must have priority over other considerations.

As Carr (2003, 2004) points out, we are now in a situation where the physical capabilities of basic IT components continue to grow at a phenomenal rate. We are not, however, seeing corresponding gains in application functionality that would, in general, justify large capital outlays to upgrade to the new equipment. Carr recommends managing the costs and risks of IT meticulously—in other words, we are no longer in a strategic situation with respect to competing on IT *hardware*.

But over and above these considerations are the ultimate value considerations: Should IT *applications* be treated as subject to the Technology Principle? The answer seems to be no, and if it is, at least part of IT has significantly different characteristics than modern technology. In fact, the *physical* components of IT—the processors, hard drives, network equipment, *are* part of modern technology, subject to growth on their own terms in accordance with the Technology Principle (and its application in Moore's Law).[2] What is revealed in the current situation is that IT *applications* are *not* automatically subject to the Technology Principle. It is not clear whether we have a choice here, but the rhythm of application development is not the rhythm of the rest of modern technology. There is no question but that Microsoft and major application developers would *like* the rhythm of application development to be the same as the rhythm of hardware development, for upgrades to be as automatic and applications to proliferate as rapidly as memory size increases. However, no amount of marketing can make something so that is just not the case.

Again, harking back to Chapter XI, software development is still nowhere near regular engineering in reliability and timeliness. It is suspicious that methods to improve productivity, although presented frequently for at least the past 30 years, have yet to get very far. In 1994, W. Wayt Gibbs documented the many ways in which software development fell short of being "software engineering," a mature discipline guaranteeing reliability. Gibbs (1994) recounts a number of spectacular disasters-outright failures and huge cost and schedule overruns—of the 1980s and 1990s.[3] He concludes: "Disaster will become an increasingly common and disruptive part of software development unless programming takes on more of the characteristics of an engineering discipline rooted firmly in science and mathematics" (p. 90).

Gibbs mentions a number of promising methodologies, as of 1994, the date of his piece. Then, in a section aptly titled "No Silver Bullets," Gibbs lists the methodologies proposed over the last 30 years to regularize software development: structured programming, CASE tools, fourth- and fifth-generation languages, object-oriented analysis, and object-oriented programming. None of these were definitively shown to improve productivity, in part because standard measures of productivity such as lines of code written per unit time are imprecise (Gibbs, 1994). The promising methodologies of 1994 were: the Capability Maturity Model (CMM), formal methods, and the clean-room approach. The CMM and clean-room approach are alive and well 10 years later, with numerous consulting companies offering instruction. Formal methods are confined to specialized academic courses, and even in 1994 Gibbs noted that reading the notation of formal methods was even harder than reading computer code. The CMM attempts to build a culture that encourages efforts to replicate quantitative and qualitative goals in software development. It prescribes evolutionary organizational behavior for the software development unit and is thus primarily a management approach. The clean-room approach attempts to apply engineering procedures, dividing the software into pathways, estimating probability of use, testing reliability, and then using the feedback to determine and improve reliability (Gibbs, 1994). Methodologies developed after 1994 include Extreme Programming and other rapid prototyping methodologies.

Although there is no question that improvement in software productivity and reliability is possible, the attempt to transform it into a branch of engineering is probably doomed to failure. For one thing, it is *provably* impossible to construct an algorithmic (i.e., calculation) procedure to find all the bugs in a computer program.[4] And the long and frustrating history to transform software development into an engineering discipline speaks for itself. So software development is probably irreducibly a craft—although there is no reason why this craft can't be managed to get more reliable results, any more than saddle building or yacht building.

But this conclusion is important for placing IT with respect to modern technology. At the heart of information technology, its development, we find something that probably does not belong to modern technology and its drive to convert the world into resources for its own use. The mystique of computer programmers about programming is legendary, and also a source of frustration for managers trying to enforce regularity and reliability.[5] I am suggesting that the mystique may have its basis in the nature of IT application development.

And, as I asserted before, although the *hardware* is part of modern technology, the *application* of that hardware to the world is not part of modern technology. I think purveyors of such cybermyths as "the singularity"—the point at which computers take over the world—being engineers, have missed the difference between progress in hardware and progress in application of hardware to the world. It is more in accordance with our everyday experience with computers that they are not that bright when applied to tasks in the everyday world. And it is a cause for praise when they do what they are supposed to with even reasonable facility and intelligence.[6]

ERP (Enterprise Resource Planning) displays one of the stigmata of modern technology, namely, its attempt to replace current business processes with a more efficient integrated process. But it also displays one of the stigmata of all application development, namely, a high failure rate. Partial completion is common, as are being over budget and behind schedule. At least one bankruptcy (FoxMeyer Drugs) has been attributed to a failed ERP implementation. And some major IT players such as Dell have aborted planned ERP implementations because the completed system would not have enough flexibility to model their businesses (Brady, Monk, & Wagner, 2001, pp. 29-31). So ERP still belongs to the world of IT applications rather than IT hardware.

IT, Species Survival, and the Ecosystem

Unfortunately, IT does seem to be neutral with respect to these two areas of ethical principles. IT is neutral with respect to whether human beings act independently in their own interests or whether they act in the best interest of the species. IT is also neutral with respect to whether the ecosystem of which we are a part can be treated as an external entity to be exploited for arbitrary human purposes. Certainly it is not part of that ecosystem.

If the human species is to have a good chance of long-term survival, we cannot be neutral on these issues. And information technology may have an important role in increasing consciousness in this area. Modern technology has already produced a globalized human species rapidly coming to share common economic and social goals. Marshall McLuhan (1964) spoke years ago of video technology producing a "global village." Information technology amplifies these effects, and they are now playing themselves out on the Internet and the World Wide Web.

The effects I have already discussed are the Web's increase in the space of personal freedom (Chapter X, E-Problems) and the offshoring of high-tech jobs (Chapter VII, Offshoring as an Ethical Issue). Thus, from an ethical point of view IT clearly contributes to the realization of the first Principle of Justice, Greatest Equal Freedom (Rawls, 1999). Yet it can also contribute to an apparent violation of the second Principle of Justice, the Difference Principle. As I concluded in Chapter VII, the issue is how to apply the Principles of Justice across societies. By globalizing commerce through the availability of information at any location, IT requires us to deal with this issue as both practical and ethical. Also, the sales tax discussion in Chapter X provides an example of how connectivity changes both practical and ethical contexts.

IT may also be able to play an important role in a background problem revealed in taking the point of view of *being* itself: Is this the best that human beings can do with the considerable talents of their species, to expand mindlessly into their environment in ways that may greatly shorten their tenure on the planet? (This is sometimes mistakenly called growth.) Or are there goals beyond this that we can adopt as a species? Right now, ethical activity incorporating consciousness of our place on the planet within the ecosystem tends to be re-active, conservative in the root sense of that word: We *refrain* from obliterating yet another piece of nature to build another suburban tract. We *limit* or *control* population. We *conserve* the environment. Indeed, such activities are of the utmost importance until such time as we figure out what we are doing as a species and what we should be doing.

We know as managers that a business without a strategic plan is a business likely to go out of control and therefore out of existence. Yet as human beings with the ability to affect the survival of all life on the planet one way or another by our activities, we do not have a strategic plan that includes the conditions for our own survival. The ultimate ethical question of how we should be using our capabilities is so far unanswered.

There have been proposals to treat the world as a business. The *New York Times* in 2003 ran an article titled, "How To Save The World? Treat It Like A Business" (Eakin, 2003). But the title turns out to be misleading. Rather than ask strategic questions about how to manage the world in a way that includes our own survival, the article reports on and recommends using market-economy entrepreneurial techniques to solve preexisting social problems, such as health insurance for low-income individuals and improving access to higher education. Such goals clearly help promote justice in our society, and innovative techniques for reaching them are laudable. But they do not bear on the larger question I am raising. Similarly, Al Gore's *Earth in the Balance* (1992), includes an excellent summary of the ecological problems that threaten long-term human existence. But, as I pointed out in the preceding chapter, Gore's message that we just need to get the economy back on track and work to avoid wasteful consumption does not address many aspects of the ecological problems now facing us.

The goals usually advocated in this area are all *enabling* ends. If realized, they will free up people to pursue their own special individual ends. But what about the species as a whole? Perhaps the closest to an end of this kind is space exploration. Although a laudable end, in a way it recommends reproducing the aimlessness and lack of direction of our species on planets other than our home planet. On this planet, a recognized difficulty in using travel to get away from one's personal problems is that one always meets oneself at the new location.[7]

One reason for attempting to formulate such species-level goals is the fact that our species will not always exist. Although I don't share a "manifest destiny" technologist's belief in the invincibility of the human species or its technology, I do hope that the human species has something like the normal two-million year life span of most species. So what will happen to our accumulated knowledge, our artworks, our buildings, our technology, our systems of communication, our social systems, our ethics, our spiritual connections, and so on? The only thing that prevents human knowledge from dying with its possessor is other human beings who are prepared to carry on the human enterprise. What meaning can it have for non-human species? Philosophers such as Kant (1787) and Wittgenstein (1953) have noted that our knowledge is in a very deep sense human knowledge, tied to the conditions of existence of human beings.[8] So it is very problematic to think of passing the torch to other species. It's not even that other species are not intelligent enough. They did not evolve together with us as part of the complex social web within which we can communicate with each other and share goals and values.

Even so, it would be by far a better goal to try to develop significant communication with other species on earth, than try to locate and communicate with species on other planets who share what can only be much fewer characteristics with us. If our knowledge can continue to survive our species, it can only be through transmission to other species, and the ones here have a lot more in common with us than any possible on another planet. There is actually some reason to believe this other than mere distance. Even on earth, when conditions are replicated as closely as possible, the same ecosystem does not replicate (Leakey & Lewin, 1995, pp. 167-170). Thus, a whole distinct chain of DNA development on some other world will probably not bear that much similarity to ours–certainly much less similarity than other intelligent species on our own world bear to us. It is significant that when extraterrestrial human species are portrayed in science fiction, we normally see recognizable human beings with heavy makeup or humanoids with large slanty eyes. If they figure in the plot, they are able to speak English, but with an accent.

One reason communication with other species seems so improbable is the tendency, partially from religion and partially from science, to see ourselves as radically different from other animals. We view other animals as having absolutely no consciousness, instead of having lesser consciousnesses. Intelligence in a species has two components: consciousness of its environment and the ability to make changes in the environment on the basis of that consciousness—and both of these at the species level. Animals may have less consciousness of their environment and less ability to make changes on the basis of that consciousness, but they do have some. Usually social animals have more ability to make changes, although conscious changes tend to be local—consider termites, bees, ants, and beavers.

Even the goal of fostering communication with other species also does not answer the question of a goal for the human species itself. The background goal is preserving whatever is worthwhile in what we have done as a species. But why and for whom? It would be hard for me to accept that in one or two million years (probably a lot sooner unless we start doing more about our relation to the environment) that all that would be left of humanity would be a lot of ruins and all the waste products of technology. The situation would be radically different from other extinct civilizations such as the Maya. There would be no other people, no anthropologists, to pick up the pieces and appreciate what had been going on.

So the question is, "What is worthwhile in what we do as a species?" And is it still worthwhile if there are no successors to appreciate it? As far as the ecosystem goes, it would be worthwhile if we did not damage it irreparably and left it capable of producing species we could recognize as our successors. Perhaps (hopefully in a million years or so) we could leave a time capsule engineered to be accessible to some future successor species.

I think it is likely that modern technology as such *won't* be a positive part of that time capsule. By modern technology, I mean the process of turning everything into resources to be used by other processes of modern technology. However, some of the products of that technology, especially IT, have a role to play in preserving ourselves and our ecosystem. The IT properties of processing speed and enormous storage make possible the modeling of complex systems involving living beings, weather, and climate. Thus, we can have a better idea of how our actions affect the other beings we share the ecosystem with. And the fact that we have a genuine worldwide communication system (the World Wide Web was accurately named with some prescience) is going to make it much easier for anyone to take the point of view of the species for ethical and value judgments.

Information Technology
and *Being* Itself

Over and above the human species and the ecosystem, we are part of the ebb and flow of *being* itself, of the coming to presence and passing away of all things. In the preceding chapter, I mentioned Heidegger's view that modern technology introduces a new way of bringing things into being that is an independent force in human existence (Heidegger, 1955). If we do not recognize the nature of this force, we will not able to place ourselves correctly. Heidegger does not believe that humanity can be the master of being, and thus the introduction by humanity of a new mode of being is inherently dangerous. Over and above any danger to the ecosystem, there is a danger of disrupting *being* itself, for there is more to *being* than the ecosystem. The ecosystem depends on the rest of what there is for its substratum.

But information technology is not modern technology. Although the *hardware* is part of modern technology, the *application* of that hardware to the world is not part of modern technology. IT *applications* do not look to reorder everything in the furtherance of their own aims. IT *applications* do not reduce everything to information; rather, they provide a separate realm where certain processes representing real objects can be carried out incredibly quickly and communicated much more easily. The tendency to confuse this parallel world with the real world was common during the heyday of the dot.com bubble. People were seriously suggesting that "mom-and-pop" local operations would need to convert to Web businesses in order to survive, that *all* commerce would be Web commerce. But IT Web applications are a parallel world, and there is no reason to expect them to replace the real world.[9]

The dot.com bubble shows us again that the course of IT is difficult to predict. Actually, it is the *application* part that is difficult; Moore's law[10] suffices for the hardware. And this is one more reason not to include the application part within modern technology. Developments as basic to IT's impact on *being* as the World Wide Web came about through very contingent circumstances. It was not an orderly research program at Microsoft or Bell Labs that produced the World Wide Web. Instead, a physicist in Switzerland developed the protocol and two graduate students at the University of Illinois produced the Web browser on university time.[11] This kind of accidental development of key IT applications is more the rule than the exception.

Because the unpredictable course of IT application development is far from over, we cannot yet definitively state the impact of IT on *being*. We have metaphors and similes, some promising and some not. To repeat, IT applications do not and cannot create a world that replaces the old one, but IT applications do seem to supply a new nervous system for connecting human beings living in that world.[12] In other words, we are able to store and access information with an ease and rapidity previously only possible within our own skins.

Another promising simile: Developing IT applications is more like art than engineering or science. As the philosopher Nelson Goodman (1976) put it: "Art is not a copy of the real world. One of the damn things is enough" (p. 3).[13] All art uses representation and expression to interpret the real world. A painting, poem, story, or musical piece has interest for us insofar as it reveals something to us about the world in which we live. But it does not *replace* anything in the real world. Artworks are thus "mostly harmless," in Douglas Adams' (1979) phrase. IT differs from art in that, although it does not replace the real world, it is intended to have a precisely defined impact on the real world. The information IT produces is used to govern real processes and to make real decisions, and thus it is not "mostly harmless." I now consider the consequence of these observations for IT professionals and managers concerned with IT.

Consequences for
IT Professional Responsibility

Because IT is not "mostly harmless," it needs to be handled with care. The previous chapters of this book have discussed the ethical impact of IT on individuals, on institutions, and on society. I will now consider two remaining ethical issues: How IT professional responsibility is manifested in issues concerning ecology and then in issues concerning *being*.

The rapid obsolescence of hardware also has ecological consequences. There are increasing problems of pollution caused by the disposal of obsolete IT hardware. For the manager or IT professional, incorporating ethical ecological concerns often comes at little cost. The ethical manager has to insure that disposal of old equipment is done in an ecologically responsible way. Provided the cost is not too great, all that is necessary is becoming aware of this responsibility.[14] If the cost is too great, then the manager or IT professional may only be able to acknowledge his support for ecological concerns. Or, in cases like these, a legislated social policy may take him off the hook by requiring compliance with ecologically safe disposal. A number of jurisdictions have standards for disposing of computer equipment in a non-polluting way, and there are numerous companies engaged in the business of safe disposal of old computer hardware.

Given that the Technological Principle still holds sway for hardware, there is no reason to believe the pace of obsolescence will change. There is nothing that a manager or IT professional can do about this. The forces involved are beyond human power. Of course, theoretically, all computer manufacturers could unanimously agree to stop improving their products. But why would they do so? From the point of view of the ecology, all that matters is that negative consequences be managed.

As far as IT *application* impacts on ecology go, attempts to streamline processes and make them more productive have the potential of benefiting the ecosystem. Reduction in the use of paper for reasons of efficiency, a common effect of the use of IT, has a positive effect in conserving forests. Although there is some offset in the environmental harm caused by the disposal of obsolete hardware, that seems to be being dealt with responsibly.

Another major important use of IT applications is in cataloguing the ecosystem. It is impossible to know what needs to preserved without accurate information about the various complex ecosystems around the planet, and the storage and processing features of IT have already proven indispensable in these areas.[15]

IT applications thus can be positive and "mostly harmless" with respect to the ecosystem.

Impacts on *Being*

From the point of view of *being*, it matters that IT hardware develops without limit. It is characteristic of modern technology to expand mindlessly for its own sake. The fact that applications are not now keeping pace with hardware improvements is not a reason to stop improving hardware. As we saw, modern technology, as a new way of bringing things into being, is not under human control. So a movement to oppose technological progress would be futile. We are now talking about hardware and not applications.

Our ethical responsibility in the face of modern technology and its Technology Principle is to give priority to the Species Survival Principle and the Ecosystem Principle. All three principles take a different form when applied to technology. The Species Survival Principle becomes: Principles of action governing the use of technology must grant considerations of the survival of the species higher priority than any individual or group interests; and the Ecosystem Principle becomes: Principles furthering the continuation of the human species must consider the survival of the ecosystem of which human beings are a part as a higher priority. The Technology Principle becomes: Technological progress is inevitable, unstoppable, and mostly beneficial. The results of technology come about through its unimpeded progress. Hence, technological development must have priority over other considerations, except for those involving the survival of the species and the ecosystem.

But, beyond this, how do we acknowledge our responsibility to *being*? Can there even be a responsibility to *being*? I think our responsibility as IT professionals and managers is to acknowledge that the Technology Principle can be constrained. From an ethical point of view, and given our biological circumstances, these constraints are expressed as the Species Survival Principle and the Ecosystem Principle. Since *being* cannot be under human control, all we may be able to do is to demonstrate our respect for the existence of concerns that go beyond our own self interest, our organizational or corporate interest, the interests of our society, the interests of our species, and the interests of our ecosystem. The ground for our respect is the fact that all of these interests are ultimately grounded in *being* in ways we may never fully understand but for which we can be grateful.

Turning to IT applications, the nature of the relation between the constructed parallel digital world and the world it represents determines the impact on *being*. This *is* a relation over which humans have control, in the way they implement IT application systems. The most immediate impact is for users of the system, who need to be treated with respect for their natures as human beings. And then, the aims of the organization need to be served by the system. Over and above that, there are considerations of whether the system furthers the aims of a just society as expressed in the Principles of Justice (Rawls, 1999). And finally, does the system respect the nature of things in the real world with which it is involved, or does it treat them only as resources to be on call for further use? For example, how is a timber management system (already adopting the point of view of modern technology, but let us ignore that for the moment) set up? Does the system record only facts useful for marketing the timber or will it also include facts about the age, beauty, and irreplaceability of this particular stand of trees, so that some of the forest can be conserved?

More generally, which data and which processes are modeled in an IT application reflect choices. Those choices reveal specific attitudes toward the user, the organization, the society, the ecosystem, and the *being* of the world the system models. It is the ethical responsibility of the IT application developer to show his or her respect for *being* and its beings in his choices.

References

Adams, D. (1979). *The hitchhiker's guide to the galaxy*. New York: Crown Publishers.

Brady, J., Monk, E., & Wagner, B. (2001). *Concepts in enterprise resource planning*. Boston: Course Technology.

Carr, N. (2003). IT doesn't matter. *Harvard Business Review* [online], May.

Carr, N. (2004). *Information technology and the corrosion of competitive advantage*. Cambridge, MA: Harvard Business School Press.

Cronenberg, D. (1999). *Existenz* [Film]. Burbank, CA: Buena Vista Home Entertainment.

Eakin, E. (2003). How to save the world? Treat it like a business. *The New York Times*, December 20, A19.

Gibbs, W. W. (1994). Software's chronic crisis. *Scientific American,* September, 86-100.

Goodman, N. (1976). *Languages of art* (2nd ed.). Indianapolis, IN: Hackett Publishing Co.

Gore, A. (1992). *Earth in the balance*. New York: Houghton Mifflin.

Heidegger, M. (1955). The question concerning technology. In *The question concerning technology and other essays,* pp. 3-36. New York: Harper & Row.

Kant, I. (1787). *Critique of pure reason*. Riga, Latvia: Hartnoch.

Leakey, R., & Lewin, R. (1995). *The sixth extinction*. New York: Doubleday.

McLuhan, M. (1964). *Understanding media*. New York: McGraw-Hill.

Rawls, J. (1999). *A theory of justice* (rev. ed.). Cambridge, MA: Harvard University Press.

Satzinger, J. W., Jackson, R. B., & Burd, S. D. (2004). *Systems analysis and design in a changing world* (3rd ed.). Boston: Thomson Course Technology.

Trakhtenbrot, B. A. (1963). *Algorithms and automatic computing machinery*. Lexington, MA: D. C. Heath Publishing.

Ullman, E. (1997). *Close to the machine*. San Francisco: City Lights Books.

Wittgenstein, L. (1953). *Philosophical investigations*. New York: Macmillan.

Young, J. (2002). *Heidegger's later philosophy*. Cambridge, UK: Cambridge University Press.

Endnotes

[1]   The goal of practitioners of Virtual Reality is to replace current reality completely. For an excellent visualization of what this would look like in a game context, see David Cronenberg's film *Existenz* (Cronenberg, 1999)

[2]   Gordon Moore, head of Intel, observed in 1965 that processor speed doubles every 18 to 24 months. This observation is called "Moore's Law".

[3]   He begins with the Denver Airport baggage handling system discussed in Chapter XI.

[4]   For the proof about just one type of bug, namely going into an infinite loop, see Trakhtenbrot (1963, 86-88).

5   For a recent example, see Ullman (1997).

6   In 2000, only 28% of projects were completed successfully (Satzinger, Jackson, & Burd, 2004, 76-7).

7   In 12-step programs, this is called a "geographic cure." It doesn't work for the reason given—the traveler is the cause of most of his own problems.

8   This is the point of Wittgenstein's enigmatic remark that if a lion could talk, we could not understand him (Wittgenstein, 1953, 223e).

9   The overreaction to the millennium bug may have depended on a similar confusion of the real world with its digital representation.

10   Gordon Moore, head of Intel, observed in 1965 that processor speed doubles every 18 to 24 months. His observation is called "Moore's Law".

11   Tim Berners-Lee at CERN developed the protocol, and Eric Bina and Marc Andreesen at University of Illinois developed the first browser, Mosaic. Napster's distributed filesharing was similarly developed in an improbable way by Sean Fanning, an undergraduate at Boston University.

12   The "nervous system" metaphor is due to Marshall McLuhan (1964), who asserted that all communications media are externalizations of our nervous systems.

13   These sentences are a quote in Goodman (1976), but he writes that he does not remember the source.

14   The cost would be too great if doing the ecologically correct thing would interfere with a manager's or an IT Professional's ability to fulfill professional duties and obligations. That includes keeping up the well-being of the organization. See Chapter II, A Background in Ethical Theory, "Rights, Duties, and Obligations."

15   See, for example, www.arkive.org/about.html.

Chapter XIV

Conclusion

Writing this book was very much a learning process for me. I began with the idea that the theories of John Rawls might be able to illuminate ethical problems involving information technology. It soon became clear to me that approaching ethics through higher level principles like those of Rawls was the correct approach. Since ethical problems of IT confront us with new situations that can't be handled in the same way as familiar cases, the only constant is the principles behind the cases.

The principle of principles that I believe regulates ethical reasoning is that higher order principles solve conflicts between lower level principles. Rawls has a powerful mechanism to generate these principles in the social realm: A social contract to follow Principles of Justice everyone would agree to from an initial position of equality. I applied Rawls' principles in social contexts after first investigating the ethical position of the IT professional. I believe that IT professionals are aware that they have distinctive ethical responsibilities, even without the benefit of a formalized professional structure of such professions as Medicine and Law. Nevertheless, as IT professional codes of conduct recognize, there can easily be conflicts between professional duty and the wider institutional context.

From a social contract point of view like Rawls', justice takes priority over efficiency, although efficiency contributes to justice. Looked at this way, corporations often seem to appear in a rather negative light. The chapters in Sections II and III exhibit Microsoft's monopolistic practices, Wal-Mart's supply-chain brutalities, the offshoring of IT jobs, and the attempts of music and movie corporations to extend copyright and legally terrorize ordinary citizens. However, when political commentators as diverse as Pat Buchanan and Ralph Nader, and the editors of *Business Week*, regularly call attention to excessive corporate power, I don't think my observations are out of place. No one would deny the economic benefits provided by corporations. But efficiency is not justice. The difficulty is that corporations are under no ethical constraints whatever and thus are no longer subject to control by individual citizens.

Rawls discusses this issue only indirectly. He was concerned about possible accumulations of political power that would greatly diminish the equality of political influence, but considered campaign finance reform as the only remediation.

In this case, one major background problem for social contract theory is that social contracts are possible only between agents with powers of the same order of magnitude. (The philosopher Thomas Hobbes is especially clear about this.) Thus, corporations are not easily included in the social contract.

Because Rawls' prime concern was principles governing political life in societies, his treatment of individual ethical rights needed to be extended to meet cases of IT ethics involving individuals. The proper ethical relation between corporations and individuals seems to me to require outside ethical constraints on corporations, precisely because they are not *ethical* individuals but only *legal* constructs. I suggested starting with very straightforward requirements such as: No killing people; no lying to cover up the corporation's mistakes; no thwarting the legitimate rights of the corporation's employees through union-busting; and complying with accepted accounting standards for truthfulness in financial reporting.

Other individual principles that extend Rawls' account include a strong Right to Privacy as developed by Justice Brandeis: Each individual has the right to keep to himself all matters not in the legitimate interest of the public. This is especially important for digital contexts and has implications for current issues such as government monitoring of e-mail, the use of RFID devices, and uniform (centralized) medical records. Other cases I discuss show that a certain amount of creativity and sensitivity is required to handle new ethical IT issues involving individuals. Sales tax collection, eliminating paper, and spam all raise new ethical considerations. This is more confirmation of my view that ethical problems in IT require going back to general principles. Rote rules just can't help much with these problems.

It is a consequence of going back to general principles that a person can often find himself in a situation where it is difficult or impossible to implement what he takes to be the correct ethical principle. This situation is a recurrent theme in this book. The appropriate models are civil disobedience for laws and partial compliance in other situations. The point is that if one thinks, as I do, that copying digital material for personal use should not be a violation of the law, then it does not follow that it is OK for me to copy it. Rather, I need to work to get the law changed—for example, by public activity such as writing about it in this book. If the possibilities of working in this way are ineffective or inappropriate because the injustice is too great and requires more immediate redress, breaking the law as a public act of civil disobedience is possible. In that case, one would first have to notify the record companies that one was doing so. Then, when they sued, one would have to willingly pay the penalty. Downloading music or movies and trying not to get caught has nothing to do with civil disobedience.

Instead, most likely one will find oneself in a situation of what I call *partial compliance*. The important thing ethically is that, even if one can't observe the ethical principle one believes is correct, one demonstrates in what one does that the correct principle exists. For example, suppose competitive pressures require a manager to offshore jobs, but he feels the practice is unjust; then, the manager may want to fund job retraining for the offshored people. Ultimately, I think this way of handling partial compliance situations is essential for ethical progress.

Considering value questions as part of ethics led me to consider the value of IT as a whole. In order to analyze value, it is essential to identify the points of view from which value is being assessed. The value of IT from the point of view of the organization and from the point of view of the economy turned out to be less connected than I expected. In fact, because of the uncertainty of socioeconomic estimates of IT value, I thought managers ought to be more concerned with the value of their own IT development projects. And even there, because of the lack of objective data on success and the difficulty in obtaining reliable value estimates, the strategic importance of projects should perhaps be a more important consideration than their expected value. In any case, the likelihood of successful completion was at least as important, and most of these important assessments from a manager's point of view within an organization require relevant experience.

To handle the analysis of value from wider points of view—the species, the ecosystem, and *being* itself—I turned to Martin Heidegger's analysis of modern technology. According to Heidegger, modern technology's distinctive features are that it is an independent force in human existence with its own point of view and its own ends, chiefly to build a new and incompatible order for the purpose of extracting and storing energy for later uses. These ends are expressed in an ethical principle I call the Technology Principle: Technological progress is inevitable, unstoppable, and mostly beneficial. The results of technology come about through its unimpeded progress. Hence, technological development must have priority over other considerations. I argued that two other principles, the Species Survival Principle and the Ecosystem Principle, should have ethical priority.

I consider IT as a special case of modern technology. Although IT hardware has the characteristics of modern technology, especially unimpeded development for its own sake, IT application development is different. IT as application is not trying to replace the world, merely to produce a useful simulation, in this respect being like art. There are ethical implications of these views for managers, the species, the ecosystem, and *being* itself. It is the ethical responsibility of the IT application developer and manager to show their respect for the species, the ecosystem, and *being* itself in their choices.

These words may seem to create a massive partial compliance problem, especially for those working in corporate environments whose (correct) principle is to maximize profits. The behavior of members of the Solidarity Union in Poland while under Soviet domination was very striking and may have been largely forgotten, yet it sets an ethical example that deserves to be remembered and imitated. When Lech Walesa was taken to prison, he did not hurl insults and vituperation in the face of his oppressors. He behaved as though he had been invited there and conducted a conversation as though he were a free man. It was this behavior that led to its being so. In other words, if you want to live in a world of truth, freedom, and justice, you can do so right now.

About the Author

Robert A. Schultz (bob.schultz@woodbury.edu, raschultz@earthlink.net) earned his PhD in philosophy from Harvard University (1971). His dissertation in ethics was under the direction of John Rawls. Schultz was a member of the philosophy faculty at the University of Pittsburgh, Cornell University, and the University of Southern California, and taught courses and published articles and reviews in the fields of ethics, logic, and aesthetics. In 1980, he assumed the position of data processing manager at A-Mark Precious Metals, a Forbes 500 company, then in Beverly Hills, CA. Since 1989, he has been professor of computer information systems and director of academic computing at Woodbury University, Burbank, CA, USA. He regularly teaches courses in database applications and design, systems development tools, and the management of information technology. He has numerous publications and presentations in the areas of database design, IT education, and the philosophy of technology.

Index

U

V

W

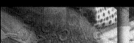